John Nicholson

The Folk Speech of East Yorkshire

John Nicholson

The Folk Speech of East Yorkshire

ISBN/EAN: 9783743384347

Manufactured in Europe, USA, Canada, Australia, Japa

Cover: Foto ©Suzi / pixelio.de

Manufactured and distributed by brebook publishing software
(www.brebook.com)

John Nicholson

The Folk Speech of East Yorkshire

THE FOLK SPEECH

OF

EAST YORKSHIRE.

BY

JOHN NICHOLSON,

Author of "Folk Moots," "Beacons of East Yorkshire," Etc.

(HON. LIBRARIAN HULL LITERARY CLUB).

LONDON : SIMPKIN, MARSHALL, AND CO.

HULL : A. BROWN AND SONS, SAVILE STREET.

DRIFFIELD : T. HOLDERNESS, "OBSERVER" OFFICE.

1889.

THOS. HOLDERNESS, PRINTER, DRIFFIELD,

TO

WILLIAM ANDREWS, Esq., F.R.H.S.,

PRESIDENT OF THE HULL LITERARY CLUB,

(1888-9),

AUTHOR OF "HISTORIC YORKSHIRE," "MODERN YORKSHIRE

POETS," ETC., ETC.,

THIS VOLUME IS RESPECTFULLY DEDICATED,

BY THE AUTHOR,

AS A TRIBUTE OF GRATITUDE

FOR THE KINDLY SYMPATHY AND ENCOURAGEMENT

WHICH HAS EVER BEEN GIVEN TO HIM,

AND WHICH FIRST INDUCED HIM

TO FOLLOW

THE PATH OF LITERATURE.

FOREWORDS.

The formation of this work has occupied my leisure moments during the last three years; and, though the publication of "Beacons of East Yorkshire" retarded its completion, it was a means of bringing me into contact with dialect-speaking people, and thus materially aiding the present work, which has formed the subject of a lecture before the Hull Literary Club; before the members and friends of the Congregational Mutual Improvement Society, Driffield; and at the Royal Institution, Hull, on the afternoon of Saturday, April the 27th, 1889.

Before the construction of roads and railways, and more perfect drainage, the towns and villages of East Yorkshire, especially in the low-lying parts, between the Wolds and the sea, were isolated and cut off from communication one with another, by the boggy marshy state of the country; and thus an archaic form of speech has been preserved. You may yet find an aged person who has never been out of the village (" toon" he very properly calls it) in which he was born. Such an one is the very incarnation of the dialect.

The Riding of the Stang (p. 8) was performed on February 18, 19, and 20, 1889, at Hedon, a small ancient borough, about five miles from Hull. A description of it, and the nominy used on that occasion, appeared in the local papers.

I have to thank Mr. Thos. Holderness, one of the authors of the Holderness Glossary, for many suggestions, and for placing at my disposal his unpublished supplement to that Glossary; also Mr. Wm. Andrews, F.R.H.S., for the loan of the engraving on p. 7; also Mr. W. G. B. Page, Sub-Librarian, Royal Institution, Hull, for compiling the Bibliography; also Mr. Geo. Lancaster, author of "Legends of Lowgate," for valuable help and kindly sympathy; and numerous friends scattered through the Riding, who have spared neither time nor trouble in gathering information for me; and the delegates of the Clarendon Press for permission to make extracts from "The York Mystery Plays."

Where requisite, the Anglo-Saxon and Old Norse ð and þ, for "th," have been used; and, where two numbers occur together, thus, 260, 143, the first refers to the page and the second to the line on that page; or, in the case of Hampole's Psalter, the first refers to the Psalm or page, and the second to the verse.

The frontispiece was obtained, through Mr. Thomas Holderness, from Mr. William Porter, Liverpool, who had it from a friend in North Jutland.

33, Leicester St., Hull.   J. N.

CONTENTS.

CHAPTER III.—SIMILES.

CHAPTER IV.—BELLICOSE WORDS.

CHAPTER V.—SPECIMENS OF THE DIALECT.

CHAPTER VI.

LIST OF ABBREVIATIONS AND OF WORKS CONSULTED.

ANDREWS. "Punishments in the Olden Time," by **Wm**. Andrews, F.R.H.S. London.

BEST. "Rural Economy in Yorkshire, in 1641." Surtees Society. 1857.

CK. BK. "Two 15th cent. Cookery Books." Editor, T. Austin, London. 1888.

CURS. MUN. "Cursor Mundi," a Northumbrian Poem. Editor, Rev. R. Morris, LL.D. London. 1874-8.

ENG. ACC. "Historical Outlines of English Accidence," by Rev. R. Morris, LL.D. London. 1879.

ENG. MIS. "An Old English Miscellany." Editor, Rev. R. Morris, LL.D. London. 1872.

ENG. PROV. "English Proverbs," by W. Carew Hazlett, London. 1882.

F. Q. Spenser's "Faerie Queene." Editor, Rev. R. Morris, LL.D. London. 1879.

GAM. "The Tale of Gamelyn." Editor, Rev. W. W. Skeat, M.A. Oxford. 1884.

HAVELOK. "Havelok, the Dane." Early English Text Society. Extra Series. London. 1868.

H. G. "A Glossary of Words used in Holderness," by T. Holderness, F. Ross, and R. Stead. English Dialect Society. London. 1877.

LAUDER. "The Minor Poems of William Lauder." Editor, F. J. Furnivall, M.A. London. 1870.

L. AND D.   "Lincolnshire and the Danes," by the Rev. G.
            S. Streatfeild, M.A.   London.   1884.
LISTER.   "A Journey to London," by Dr. Martin Lister.
            1628.
MICRO.   "Micro-cosmographie," by John Earle.   London.
            1628.
PER. REL.   Percy's "Relics of Ancient Poetry."   Warne,
            London.   1880.
P. P.   "Piers Plowman."   Editor, Rev. W. W. Skeat,
            M.A.   Oxford.   1881.
PR. OF CON. Hampole's "Pricke of Conscience."   Editor, Rev.
            R. Morris.
PR. TR.   Hampole's "Prose Treatises."   Editor, Rev. G.
            G. Merry, M.A.   London.   1866.
PSAL.   Hampole's "Psalter."   Editor, Rev. H. R.
            Bramley, M.A.   Oxford.   1884.
R. R.   "Ratis Raving."   Editor, J. Rawson Lumby,
            M.A.   London.   1870.
SH. CAL.   Spenser's "Shepheard's Calender."   Editor, Rev.
            R. Morris, LL.D.   London.   1879.
SKEAT.   "An Etymological Dictionary of the English
            Language," by Rev. W. W. Skeat, M.A.
            Oxford.   1882.
SPENSER.   "The Works of Spenser."   Globe Edition.
            Editor, Rev. R. Morris, LL.D.   London. 1879.
STEPHENS.   "Runic Monuments," by Professor George
            Stephens.   London.   1866.
WIC.   Wicliffe's "Bible."   Editors, Forshall and Mad-
            den.   Oxford.   1850.
YORK PL.   "York Mystery Plays."   Lady Editor, Miss
            Lucy Toulmin Smith.   Oxford.   1885.

FOLK SPEECH OF EAST YORKSHIRE.

CHAPTER I.

INTRODUCTORY.

Introduction. The folk speech of East Yorkshire is almost untrodden literary ground. It is not, and has not been, used much by writers : it is only spoken, and that by decreasing numbers. Railways, telegraph, and School Boards — steam, electricity, and education—are surely killing dialects, even though of late years, much attention has been directed to their preservation in Glossaries and dictionaries—perservation in books, as antiquarian discoveries.

Though our dialect is rich in vigorous words, and is capable of expressing humour, pathos, sarcasm, and philosophy, in its own peculiar way, we possess no literature such as is produced in the West Riding and Lancashire ; and we have no writers like Ben Preston, John Hartley, or Edwin Waugh. We have hitherto been restricted to Glossaries, and to an occasional fugitive piece in the columns of the local newspapers or magazines.

In East Yorkshire there is only one large town, and that, being a sea-port, is cosmopolitan, and contains but a small percentage of dialect-speaking people, so that, scarcity of population, and the absence of "touch" between current literature and the dialect speakers, may be assigned as probable reasons why there is a dearth of dialect literature. With ten or twelve large, busy, wealthy manufacturing centres distributed through the Riding, there would doubtless be both a demand for, and a supply of, dialectic writings and publications.

Before the Norman Conquest there were two History. dialects in England —Northern and Southern. Both these dialects were greatly affected where they came into contact with the Midland dialect, which, rising into prominence after the Norman Conquest, has ultimately become our standard English. Had York become the metropolis, instead of London, standard English would have been different, in many things, to what it is now.

The Northern dialect was spoken in Yorkshire, Durham, Northumberland and the Lowlands of Scotland; and the folk speech of East Yorkshire presents characteristics which were marks of the old Northern dialect, most particularly in the inflection of the verb, present indicative singular—

Northern 1st pers hope or hopes, East Riding (ah) hooap-*es*

     ,,   2nd ,, hop *es*   ,,   (thoo) hooap-*es*

     ,,   3rd ,, hop *es*   ,,   (he) hooap-*es*

also in the present indicative plural ; for the Northern dialect had such forms as—kinges ride*s* ; fisches ete*s* ; while an East Yorkshire man might say "Them as say*s* seeah, tell*s* a big lee (lie)." The Northern dialect often had the guttural *k* where *ch* is now found—kaff (chaff); kist (chest). And this accounts for many of the double forms in modern English, as *ditch* and *dike*, *pouch* and *poke*, *church* and *kirk*, &c.

The Holderness dialect bears one mark of Antiquity. antiquity. It has no definite article, while all other parts of Yorkshire have either the word in its entirety, or contracted to "t" (towd man) or "th" (thowd man) or modified into "d" (he went intid hoose). Professor Stephens * says that the article is unknown on the very oldest Runic monuments, as well as in the oldest Scandinavian dialects and the oldest English.

In the dialect strong forms of past tenses abound : thus— he *clam* (climbed) three like a squerril. He *dhrade* (dreaded) maisther gettin ti knaw. We *grov* (graved, dug) that piece o' grund ower last neet. Lads *mew* (mowed) 12 acre afooar dinner. It *snew* (snowed) heavy last neet; an this mooanin snaw *clov* (cleaved, stuck) like cobbler wax.

Yorkshire and Lincolnshire became so much
Danish Influence.   subject to the influence of the Northmen that they were divided into Wapentakes and Ridings, as their own country over the sea was. Place names and personal names (such as Thirkell, Straker, Trigg, Dring, Lill, Tock, Stott, Beal, Swain, Dougall, Brand, Ross, Seward) in abundance, prove their ascendancy ; and in East Yorkshire, the battles of Stamford Bridge certainly, and Brunanburh probably, were fought.

The frontispiece shews how closely the dialects of East Yorkshire and Jutland are similar, and the Rev. J. C. Atkinson † has shewn how much the Cleveland and Jutland dialects are alike; and the Rev. G. S. Streatfeild's "Lincolnshire and the Danes," shews what influence they exercise there. These Northmen have given to standard English such words as are, bask, scud, &c., and to our dialects beck, garth, gate (way) middin, rafter, sen or sin (self), flick (flitch) and scores more.

The dialect is rich in meaning and in numbers
Wealth.   of words. In modern English, we still retain "*daft*," but where are daffen, daffener, daffenin, daft-like, dafty, daft-heead, daftish, and daftness. We still retain *gobble*, but where are gob, gobbet (Spenser)

---

* Runic Monuments, p. 30.   † Glossary of Cleveland.

gobbler, gobful, goblock, gob-fight (fight with words from the mouth) gob-sludge, gob-stick, and gob-meeat?

How good such words as these are :—lowth (lowness) fulth (fulness) growsome (favourable to growth) laboursome, healthsome, lithesome, contracted to lissom; betterment, botherment, oddment, muckment, messment.

Force.   Dialectic speech is vigorous and forceful.

(*a*) A cake is left too long in the hot oven. Is it simply burnt or scorched? Oh, no! *It's* getten *fire-fanged.*

(*b*) A new hat has been soaked by a heavy shower of rain. It is not simply spoiled, but "all *mense* is off it," an expression which will compare most favourably with its modern equivalents—all the gilt is off the ginger-bread, or the bloom is off the peach.

(*c*) Said a sympathiser to a friend in trouble "If Ada dees, Ah think thoo'll sluf thi heart oot." Compare this with being broken hearted, or eating your heart out.

(*d*) The word "dowly" is very expressive. If the morning be wet and miserable, with no sign of amendment, here is "a *dowly* leeak oot." A sick person is weak, and lonely, and sad, and is "varry *dowly*" when a friend calls. A lonely, gruesome spot, is a *dowly* spot, and a dispirited person is said to be *dowly*, and carrying that look, "hez a *dowly* leeak aboot him."

(*e*) A hawker is a "run-aboot man"; and a morose cross-grained person is "rusty." A huge roaring fire is "up ti galli-balk" the balk or beam on which the *reckons* are hung. A person who uses filthy language is a "muck-spoot," and a silly foolish person is an "otther-pooak," that is a poke or sack of otther (nonsense).

(*f*) A piece of fallen wick in a candle flame, which causes the tallow to run to waste, is a "thief"; and a thoroughly forlorn despairing man is said to be a "hing lug;" while an old woman who dresses like a young girl, is said to be "a awd yow i' lamb fashion."

(*g*) What wisdom and philosophy there is in styling one who spends his whole life in hoarding riches, a "yath worrum"; that is an earth worm.

(h) "Heead-wark's as laboursome as backwark" is the dialectic method of saying that brain work is as hard as hand work.

Humour.
(1) As the days in spring time are lengthening, they are said to be getting "a cock sthraade (stride) langer noo."

(2) If, in making dough, the good wife should put too much water, she has "dhroondid minler" (drowned the miller); and there are those living who had no yeast in their younger days, but used sour dough to leaven the bread. So Wicliffe translates the well-known text " Beware of the *sour dough* (leaven) of the Pharisees."

(3) Out of the carrs, black timber is often obtained, and is known as Awd Nooah (old Noah); the mouth is a "tatie thrap" (pŏtatoe trap), and the throat is a "reead looan," (red lane).

(4) The narrow spaces allowed for eaves droppings, between houses, is known as a "dog loup" (dog leap or jump).

(5) Should any one boast of his horsemanship, he is quietly asked if he can "sit fling;" and one who is thoroughly beaten in an argument is sent away " wiv a lop iv his lug," (a flea in his ear).

(6) " Well, Jack," said one man to another, "did tha hev a good tuck oot (feast) at your young maisther's weddin?" " Nay, nut mich! They meead ma tēe up pooak afore it was full."

(7) One who is working in vain, or receiving no pay, is trying "ti wakken a deead oss " (to awaken a dead horse).

(8) Said one woman to another, "Ah gat sike a *callin* as Ah nivver had i' mi life. She called ma ivvery thing at she thowt bad ! "

" Why ! nivver mind, lass, what she *calls* tha, seeah lang as
she disn't *call* tha ower leeat fo' dinner."

Expressions such as these only skim the surface of the
subject. A whole volume could be devoted to the humour
of the dialect, for a native cannot speak many words without
giving utterance to some droll expression.

In comparing the dialects of Yorkshire, the great difference which strikes a listener is the vowel sounds, a difference
so marked that a river, a valley, a range of hills, another
township, shall cause or give another pronunciation of the
same word. The majority of words is common to all
northern dialects, but this variation of vowel sounds makes
the dialect of a district almost as different as another
language. Thus, in East Yorkshire, the word home, is
ham in place names, *yam* in some districts, *wom* in others ;
hooam in others ; and *heeam* in others.

Our standard English could be enriched by an infusion of
some of our dialect words—words that are native, expressive,
exact, and elegant—words properly formed, easily understood, having life in them.

Printing has congealed and embalmed words, but there
are dialect words in existence as well worth recording and
preserving as any that have ever appeared in type—dialect
words which would well serve their users, ere they lost their
force, and became as empty shells from which the life had
departed.

RIDING THE STANG.

CHAPTER II.

NOMINIES.

The word nominy is in use, both in the East and West Ridings, and its meaning in both is the same. A prepared oration, or a set speech or form of words, is a nominy. The town crier and the church clerk use nominies.

It was a village lovefeast, and, of the two speakers, one was eloquent and fluent, while the other was all hesitation. The former was said "ti knaw his nominy, like a chotch clerk; bud tuther chap hadn't getten his nominy off, an' hackered an' stammered aboot, whahl yan cud mak nowt o' what he said."

When boys go Christmas boxing they have a set form of words :

> Ah wish ya a Merry Chris'mas and a Happy New Year ;
> A pocket full o' munny an' a cellar full o' beer ;
> Two fat pigs, an' a new-coved coo ;
> Good maisther and misthress hoo di ya do.
> Pleease will ya gi' ma a Chris'mas box ?

Should the boy be unable to recite this rhyme, he would be told he " didn't knaw his nominy," and would be sent away empty-handed.

The village is in an uproar. The very sparrows, by their lively movements and twittering, and the rooks, in the rookery bordering one side of the village green, by their wheeling flight and incessant cawing and clamouring, seem to partake of the common excitement. A throng of men and boys, aye, and women too, some with sticks and some with old tins and pans, are as eager as bees at swarming time ; and are talking long and loud, with faces red with excitement and intensity of purpose. Jack Nelson has cruelly beaten his wife, a gentle, noble, uncomplaining woman, always willing to help a neighbour ; but, alas ! as is too often the case, united to a wretch, whom to call a brute, would be to degrade the brute creation.

So now public opinion is roused, and Jack must be taught that the whole community disapproves of his cruelty, and if it cannot punish, at least it will endeavour to shame him.

An effigy of Jack is tied on a stang (a long pole, though most frequently a ladder) and carried by two men through the village, accompanied by a motley crowd, with instruments more famed for sound than music. A drum is a decided acquisition, and he who has a horn is envied by those who have nothing more melodious than a tin whistle, an old kettle, or their own hoarse voice. So on the grand procession sweeps, to halt before Jack's door, when at a given signal all instrumental music (?) is hushed, while the vocalists have their turn. With voices loud and harsh, they break out

Here we cum, wiv a ran a dan dan;
It's neeather fo' mah cause nor tha cause that Ah ride this stang,
Bud it is fo' Jack Nelson, that Roman-nooased man.
Cum all you good people that live i' this raw,
Ah'd he' ya tak wahnin, fo' this is oor law;
If onny o' you husbans your gud wives do bang,
Let em cum to uz, an we'll ride em the stang.
He beat her, he bang'd her, he bang'd her indeed;
He bang'd her afooar sha ivver stood need.
He bang'd her wi' neeather stick, steean, iron, nor stower,
Bud he up wiv a three-legged stool an knockt her backwards ower.
  Up stairs aback o' bed,
  Sike a racket there they led.
  Doon stairs, aback o' deer,
  He buncht her whahl he meead her sweear.
Noo,'if this good man dizzant mend his manners,
The skin of his hide sal gan ti the tanner's;
An if the tanner dizzant tan it well,
He sal ride upon a gate spell;
An if the spell sud happen ti crack,
He sal ride upon the devil's back;
An if the devil sud happen ti run,
We'll shut him wiv a wahld-goose gun;
An if the gun sud happen ti miss fire,
Ah'll bid ya good neet, for Ah's ommast tired.

The instrumentalists, jealous at their enforced silence, now burst in with an united blast; not a bad representation of musical chaos. And so, with cheering and loud noise, Jack's effigy is carried round the village, for three successive nights, and finally burned in a huge bonfire on the village green. (Ridden in Hedon, 18th, 19th, and 20th, February, 1889.)

The time is early autumn; the scene a field of ripening turnip seed. Perched on the top of a five-barred gate is a young urchin, bareheaded and energetic, armed with an instrument shaped like a capital Y. Across the top of the Y is stretched a wire, on which are threaded several pieces of sheet iron, about two or three inches square. He is a "bod-tenther" (bird-tender); and, seeing a flock of finches alighting on the ripening seed, he seizes his rattle, shakes it vigorously, and raises his young shrill voice into a sing-song rhyme :

> Shoo way, bods! Shoo way, bods!
> Tak a bit, an leeave a bit,
> An nivver cum ne ma'e bods.

This is his work; and he marches about, singing and shaking his rattle, while the sounds he produces melt away into the natural surroundings, and help to give tone and formation to what we know as "country sights and sounds."

In the centre of a village green stands the village cross; and on the steps of this cross two or three boys have met. They have been "bod-nestin" (bird-nesting); and are comparing quantities and specimens. Several more boys are about the place, playing at "merrills," or "Jack steean," or cricket, with a pile of old tins for a wicket. The harmony of the whole scene is broken in upon, by one of the bird-nesters exclaiming, in a loud surprised tone, "Ah tell tha, it's a robin egg!" "It isn't!" "It is!" and so the dispute waxes warmer, till all the others leave their sport to become judges. Their decision is that one of the nesters has robbed a robin's nest—a shameful act, which meets with summary jurisdiction, whether done ignorantly or not. They all draw

together from him, point their fore fingers at him, hiss and
boo, and finally break into a singing rhythm,

> Robin takker, robbin takker,
> Sin, sin, sin!

repeated again and again, with increasing volume and
vehemence as others join in the fray, until the offender is
driven away. To effect this, his persecutors not unfrequently
take their caps, or knot their handkerchiefs, and "mob" him
for his cruelty to the bird they protect.

Boys have also a similar punishment for those who "blab"
secrets. Should a boy have betrayed an intended raid on a
neighbour's orchard, or told who chalked a life-size caricature
of the school-master on the door of the school porch, or told
who had rung the church bell in the middle of the night,
after putting a tub full of water before the doors of those
likely to rush out to see what was the matter—such an one
was hissed at, hooted at, pointed at, and finally driven away,
his tormentors singing

> Tell pie tit
> Laid a egg an' couldn't sit!

On New Year's day it is a custom at Driffield for the
boys of the town to assemble in the main street, go in
disorderly rout to the shops of the chief tradesmen, and,
standing in the road before each shop, sing out:

> Here we are at oor toon end,
> A shooldher o mutton, an a croon ti spend.
> **Hip! hip! hooray!**

until some of the stock of the tradesman is thrown to them and scrambled for.

The Flambro' children, who run after the vehicles which convey visitors to and from their picturesque neighbourhood, have a variation of this rhythm—

> Here we are at oor toon end,
> A bottle o' gin, and a croon ti spend.
> If ya hain't a penny, a hawp'ny 'll do ;
> If ya hain't a hawp'ny, God bless you!
> Hip! hip! hooray!

The bringing home of the last load of harvest is always a joyous time. At Bilton, when the harvest is safely gathered in, the whole village gives itself up to merriment and festivity. A half-holiday is given to all employees, and they, one and all, enter into sports and joyous holiday-making. But now one scarcely ever hears of the harvest song that used to be sung when the last load entered the well-filled "stagga'th," and when the younger people "scram'led" for nuts and apples. Then, the master, or foreman, entering the stack-garth at the horses' head, began,

> Here we are, as tite (from Ice. tittr, soon) as nip,
> We nivver flang ower bud yance iv a grip,
> An then oor Jack gav her the slip.
> Hip! hip! hooray!

[Great effort has been made to get the completion of this song, but hitherto without success].

The harvest is all gathered in, the "stagga'th" is full of "pikes" and stacks, and has overflowed into the home field;

for the crops have been heavy, and there is no sign of "deaf" ears in the heavy "shavs." For some days, boys have been "dhrawin sthreeah" (that is, pulling straw out by handfuls from the straw stack made last thrashing day) and laying it straight in bundles ready for the "theeaker," who takes a bundle at a time, and after spreading some of it as evenly as possible, "keeams" (combs) it, by means of a "stower" (staff) having for teeth, long nails driven through it.

The thatcher is busy at work. The only sounds which break the silence are the occasional strokes of his "keeàm," as he apostrophises some mislaid straw which is difficult to get right. By and by there is a sound of children's voices, playing "heddo" (hide oh!) among the straw, and behind the stacks and buildings. They soon discover the thatcher, and their shrill voices are raised to chant a nearly-obsolete rhythm—

Theaker, theaker, theake a span
Come off yer lather, an' hang yer man.

And should the "theaker" enter into the fun, he would reply

When my maisther hes thetched all his streeah
He will then cum doon an' hing him that says seeah.*

Two chubby little fellows are going down a country lane. A heavy shower has just ceased, but there are few pools, for the parched earth has sucked up the summer rain, and were it not for the scent-laden air, and the liquid gems that bedeck every blade of grass and jewel every spray, you would scarcely know that a welcome down-pour had cooled the land, for the sun is shining brightly, and the sky is blue overhead. From the topmost twig of an ash tree, a blackbird is pouring forth his flute-

*Best's Rural Economy, p. 147.

like notes, and the pauses in his hymn of praise, almost as
eloquent as his song, are filled in by the shriller tones of the
thrush, the lively chatter of the whitethroat, the sweet ditty
of the hedge-sparrow, the chirp of the homely sparrow, or
the tiny squeak of the shrew as it rustles through the wet
grass.   High overhead, a skylark is heard but not seen, and
its silvery notes ripple through the warm air, already
becoming misty, the effect of sun and rain.

The boys are seemingly heedless of these things, for their
eyes are bent earthward, and they have difficulty in preventing
their feet from crushing the numerous black slugs that are
crawling over the ground, leaving a slimy track behind them.
These they avoid, but noting a small snail, looking over-
burdened and top heavy by its cream and brown shell, one
of them seizes it by its house, and lifts it up.   In an instant
it has drawn within its shell, and squeezes itself tight and
close, as they poke it with a blade of sword-grass.   As their
efforts to dislodge it make it withdraw within its shell more
and more, they threaten it thus :—

> Sneel, sneel, put oot yer hoan (horn)—
> Or Ah'll kill yer fayther and muther te moan (to-morrow);

but, being unsuccessful in their repeated efforts to dislodge
it, they throw it away, and then pretend to read their future
occupation or condition by picking off the spikelets of the
flower stalk of the piece of grass.   Beginning at the lowest
one, they take off one for each trade or condition—

> Tinker, tailor, soldier, sailor,
> Rich man, poor man, beggar man, thief ;

and that which falls to the last or topmost spikelet represents
what they will be when they are to manhood grown.

Noon has passed, and the baby, after a fretful and wakeful

night, is only awaking, but bright and refreshed. The nurse takes him, and, swinging him in her arms, keeps time to the following nursery rhyme—

> Pranky iddity; pranky aye,
> Baby hezn't been pranked ti-day,
> But let ti-morra come ivver sa soon
> Baby sall be pranked bi noon.

Except in this simple ditty, the word *prank* is obsolete. It is, however, used by Spenser.

"Some prancke (trimmed) their ruffes," (F. Q. Bk. 1. c. 4).

"In sumptuous tire she joy'd herselfe to *prank.*" (F. Q. Bk. 2. c. 2).

Iddity is also obsolete. It is a compound of Old English dihtan, to dress, deck, or adorn ; and the A.S. prefix *ge*, corrupted to "*i*."

"Soon after them, all dauncing in a row,
The comely virgins came, with girlands *dight.*" (F. Q. Bk. 1. c. 12).

"I *dighte* me derely, and dide me to chirche." (P. P. 1. 12. 963).

CHAPTER III.

SIMILES.

Until attention is drawn to the fact, few people seem to be aware how much simile and metaphor enter into our common speech. Likeness and figure are familiar in our mouths as household words ; and, in some respects a simile is like a proverb, for it often contains the wisdom of many in the wit of one. Among common East Riding similes may be mentioned the following :—

As awd as mi tongue, an' a bit awdher then mi teeth.

As black as a craw. Crows in the East Yorkshire are "greybacks" and rooks are "craws." Hence the simile.

As black as hud. Hud is the hob of a fireplace.

As black as thunner. (thunder).

As blind as a bat. Doubtless so thought because of the apparently aimless flight of the "flitter-moose" as it is frequently called.

As blue as a whetstan. Blue is the Conservative colour in East Yorkshire, so that to say "He's as blue as a whetstan" means he is a Conservative. But when anyone is blue with cold, they are also said to be as blue as a whetstan. Whetstan is the stone on which tools are whetted or sharpened.

As blithe as a lennit (linnet).

As brade as narra, like Paddy's plank. The common version is "as broad as long."

As brant as a hoose sahd. Brant means steep, upright, high, as applied to rocks, hills, &c. So, of one who has a high forehead it is said, "His broo's (brow is) varry *brant.*" As one who is vain and conceited holds his head high, so it is said of such an one " He walks as *brant* as a pisimire." (red ant).

As breet as sun.

As breet as silver.

As breet as a button, or a new pin.

As breet as a bullace. The "bullace" is the fruit of the wild plum, and only those who know how bright it will become by being well rubbed can understand and appreciate the simile. — 15th Cent. Cook, Bk., p. 24. "Take fayre *bolasse* wasshe hem clene, and in wyne boyle hem."

As broon as a berry.

As bug (vain, proud, elated) as a lad wiv a leather knife.

As bug as a dog wi' two tails.

As bug as a cheese.

As cawd (cold) as ice.

As cawd as deeath.

As clean as a whistle. Clean means complete, perfect, or clear, and refers to the sound made by the whistle, and not to the whistle itself. Just as in "as clear as a bell," the word *clear* refers to the sound, and not to the instrument causing the sound.

" Lat it boyle wyl, but loke þat it be *cline* rennyng (clean running)." (15 cent. Cookery Book, 31, 14.)

As croose (lively) as a loose (louse) or lopp (flea).

As cross as a wasp.

As dark as pick (pitch). Always used adverbially in connection with "dark."

As dark as bellas. Is this "bell hoose"? For belfrys are nearly always dark places.

As deead as a deear nail. In Piers Plowman (P. 14, l. 185)

B

it reads "as ded as a dore tree" where *tree* means simply *wood*.

As deead as a herrin.

As deeaf as a yat stowp (gate post).

As deep as Garrick. This seems to be well-known all over the country, for it is current in Cornwall and Wales. *

As deep as a well.

As deep as Awd Nick.

As dhry as a cassan. The cassan was a cake of dried cow's dung, used as fuel. It was formed either by *casting* the soft dung against a wall, from which it could easily be detached when dry; or it was spread, two or three inches thick, on a piece of level ground, and cut into squares, oblongs, diamonds, or other shapes, at the pleasure of the maker. When dry, it was stacked or stowed away ready for use. A fire made of cassans and chalk stones burnt well and long, giving off great heat, little smoke, and a pleasant perfume.

As dhry as a kex. The kex is the dried stalk and seed-pod of the poppy, &c.

As eeazy as a awd shoe.

As fat as a pig.

As fat as a match dipt at beeath ends. The present paraffin match has quite superseded the old brimstone match, made of a splinter of wood about six inches long, and dipped at both ends. They used to be hawked about by pedlars, and sold at a halfpenny per bundle of about 20 matches; and were only used for ignition by the spark on the tinder, produced by the flint and steel.

As fast as a thief iv a mill. The mill referred to would be one of the old wooden wind-mills, built on posts, with only one way of ingress and egress, and which could easily be surrounded, thus giving no chance of escape to the thief therein.

* Hazlitt's English Proverbs, p. 65.

As fit as a flea.   As ready and eager as a flea for blood.

As flat as a pan-keeak (cake).

As fond (silly, foolish) as a billy gooat.

As fond as a jackass.

As fond as a geease (goose) stuck i' heead.

As fond as Dick's hat-band, at went roond his hat nahn tahms (nine times) an then wadn't tee (wouldn't tie). This, slightly varied in form, appears to be widely circulated. *

As full as a egg's full o' meeat.

As full as a tick.   A *tick* is a sheep-louse, which has always a full bloated appearance.

As good as ivver stepped upo' shoe leather.

As good as they mak em.

As green as gess (grass).

As grey as a badger.

As green as a yalla cabbish (cabbage).   This saying is used when anyone assumes innocence or ignorance.   " Take faire *Cabochis*, pike hem, and wash hem, and parboyle hem," (15 cent. Cook. Bk., 69, 32).

As hahd as nails.   ⎫
As hahd as a brick. ⎬ Said of persons.
                     ⎭

As hahd as a grund tooad.

As happy as days is lang.

As heavy as leead.

As holla as a dhrum.

As hungry as a hunther.

As keeal (cool) as a coo-cummer (cucumber).

As keen as musthad.

As kittle as a moose-thrap.   For *kittle*, see Glossary.

As lang as a fiddle.   Said of one who goes about with a long melancholy face.

As lazy as a hoond.

As leet (light) as a feather.

_____

* Hazlitt's English Proverbs, p. 75.

As mad as a March hare.

As mucky as muck. Said of dirty roads, &c.

As mischievous as a munkey. Applied to children.

As many lives as a cat.

As nice as nice could be.

As pawky as yo' pleease. *Pawky* means impudent.

As peart as a lop. (flea).

As poor as a chotch moose.

As ram as a awd fox. It is this *ram* or strong fœtid smell which furnishes the " scent " for the fox-hounds.

As reead (red) as a blud puddin.

As reead as rudd. Rudd is a material used by housewives to ruddle (redden) the brick floors of their kitchens, &c.

As rotten as pash, *i.e.*, as rotten as rotten can be, all broken up and decayed.

As rough as a badger.

As roond as a ball.

As sackless as a goose. *Sackless* means witless, foolish.

As scrugded as three iv a bed.

As shahp as a rezzil. A *rezzil* is a weasel.

As shahp as a needle. Sharp, the opposite of blunt.

As shahp as leetnin. Sharp, the opposite of slow.

As sad as a dumplin. Heavy clayey land is said to be *sad*. So Wicliffe (Luke vi., 48.) " It was foundid on a *sad* stoon."

As slape as glass, (or ice, or an eel). Boys like ice to be *slape*, *i.e.* slippery, for then they can *slither* or slide well.

As slaw as a sneel (snail). See Nominies, p. 14.

As small as a sparrable.

As smooth as velvit.

As snog as a bug iv a rug.

As soft as a boiled tonnap (turnip). Said of any person who easily gives way to tears. A boy who cries for a little, or who is cowardly, is sure to have this simile contemptuously thrown at him.

As soor as a crab.   A crab is a wild apple.

As soor as vahjas.   Hazlitt's English Proverbs, p. 77, gives "As sour as verjuice (or vargeis). *Leeds.* Verjuice is the juice of crabs or sour apples. "Caste thereto pouder ginger, *vergeous,* salt, and a littul safferon." 15th Cent. Cookery Book, p. 72.

As sthreyt as a bolt.   A bolt is an obsolete weapon, a knob-headed arrow for a cross-bow.

As sthreyt as a yard o' pump wather.

As still as a moose.

As stoddy as a awd yow (ewe).

> Many frosts, and many thowes
> Make many rotten *yowes.*—Hazlitt's Proverbs, p. 285.

As stunt as a mule.   *Stunt* means obstinate, dogged, and is a form of *stint.*

As reet (right) as a thrivet.

As sweet as hunny.

As sweet as a nut; where *sweet* means sound and whole-some.   Thus manure, or land, in good condition, is said to be *sweet.*

As thick as inkle weeavers.

As threw as Ah's standin here.

As tite as nip.   See Nominies, p. 12.   In Hampole's Psalter there are many instances of this word "tite" from Ice. tittr, soon.   A *nip* is that which is done quickly.   To *nip up* to a place is to go nimbly.   "If thou here noghte als (hear not so) *tyt* i sall noghte leue." (believe) Ps., v., 3. "He helpis noght als *tyte* as men." Ps. ix, 22. "Als *tite* i cum to deme." (judge) Ps. xi, 5.   "For thou gifes noght als *tite* as thai wild." Ps., xxiv, 6.

As teeaf as wesh-leather.

As teeaf as rag-lad (gristle).   The peculiar cartilage to which this is applied will split into filaments or "tags," hence it is termed "teeaf-tags."

As thick as a booad.   Equivalent to "as big as a lump of chalk."

As thin as a wafer.

As thrang as Throp's wife.   Hazlitt's Proverbs, p. 80, gives "As thrang as Thrap's wife, as hanged hersell i' t' dish-clout."

As wake as a kitlin.   Wake—weak; kitlin—kitten.

As wet as a dishcloot.

As wet as thack.   Thack—thatch.

As white as dhrip.   Dhrip, from Ice. dript, a snow-drift. Said of things.

As white as a mauk.   Mauk—maggot.   Said of persons.

As yalla as brimston.

He dances aboot *like a scoperil* (a child's teetotum).

It sticks *like a burr.*   The burr is the round seed of the hairiff, or goose-grass; and children, in play, often take a long spray of it, and lay it on the dress of a companion, where it will adhere closely.   They call it "having a sweetheart."

Ah sweeats *like a brock.*   The brock is a small green insect (cicada spumaria) which exudes a white froth-like moisture, commonly known as "frog-spit."

It stinks *like a fummat,* i.e. a polecat.

CHAPTER IV.

BELLICOSE WORDS.

The dialect of East Yorkshire contains, in great abundance, words expressing fighting or quarrelling, either by words, limbs, or instruments. The following list, lengthy though it be, does not profess to be complete.

Bam, to brow-beat. "Ah couldn't get a wod in neeah hoo, that lawyer chap *bammed* ma seeah."

Bash, to bang, to clash together. "He *bashed* lad's heead ageean deear powst."

Baste, (Ice. beysta, to beat), to flog. "Ah'll *baste* tha weel, if thoo dizzn't mahnd what thoo's deeahin."

Bat, a rap, a blow. "Give him a *bat* ower heead for his pawk." (impudence).

Bats, a beating. "Thoo'll get thi *bats*, mi lad, when thi fayther comes yam." (home)

Bell Tinker, a chastisement "Ah'll gi tha *bell tinker* if thoo disn't mahnd what thoo's aboot!"

Beltin, a flogging with a belt. Query—Is "bell tinker" a beltinger?

Bencillin, a beating. "Tom gav his lad a good *bencillin* for steealin taties."

Bray, to flog, to chastise; literally, to crush. Said a man who discovered his son cheating and lying, "Ah'll *bray* him black and blew wi besom shaft." "Take almaundys and

blaunche hem þan *bray* hem in a mortere." (15th Cent.
Cookery Book, p. ˙30, l. 10.)

> Yone boy with a brande
> *Brayed* me full well.—York·Pl., 259, 143.

Bunch, (1) to kick. "Bunch him, Ned ; he sed thoo
was a feeal ;" (2) a kick. "He ga' ma a *bunch* ower mi
leg." "Ah's nut boon ti he' mah lad *buncht aboot* like that ;
Ah 'll tak him away."

It was an assault case at the Driffield Police Court :

Magistrate, (to Plaintiff) : Well, my good woman, what
did she do ?

Plaintiff (indignantly) : Deeah ? Why ! sha clooted mi
heead, rove mi cap, lugged mi hair, dhragged ma doon, an
buncht ma when Ah was doon.

Magistrate (piteously and amazedly) to Clerk : What did
she say ?

Clerk (slowly and decisively) : She says the defendant
clooted her heead, rove her cap, lugged her hair, dhragged
her doon, an buncht her when sha was doon.

As he ended the court revelled in laughter for a short time.

Said a labourer, to a man who wished to cross a field,
"Y'u can gan across that clooase, only mahnd an deean't
bunch tonnaps up."

Bung up, to close as with a *bung*. "Bung his ees up for
him, he desahves it."

Bussel, to drive away angrily. "Noo, away wi y'u ; or
Ah 'll *bussle* ya off i' quick sticks."

Callitin-Boot, a wordy quarrel.

Cawk, to flog. Hence "cawkin" a flogging.

Catch it, to meet with punishment. "Thoo 's gannin ti
catch it, mi lad."

Cherrup, a sharp blow. "Ah 'll gie tha a *cherrup* ower
lug, an then thoo 'll mebby think o' what thoo 's tell'd."

Chin Chopper, a blow on the jaw or under the chin.

Chip, a slight quarrel. "We 've nivver had a *chip* sin we
wer wed."

Clap, (Ice., klappa, to pat) a stroke with the flat hand, or some broad instrument, so that a noise is made by the stroke. "*Clap* his lugs for him."

Clash, a violent knock against a hard substance. "Bob *clasht* Jack's heead an wall tegither."

Cloot, (Ice. klutr—rag) to strike as with a cloth—"*Cloot* him weel."

Crawk, a knock on the head. "He gat sike a *crawk* wi cunstuble's staff."

Crack, a stunning blow. "Ah fetched him a *crack*."

Cob, a kick with the knee, instead of the foot.

Cuff, literally, a blow with the cuff or fore arm; most frequently on the head.

Dab, a stroke in the face. "Jack gav him a *dab* iv his ee."

Daffener, a stunning blow. "Ah ga ratten a *daffener* wi mi speead, an then Ah killed it." Used also as a verb; "He *daffen'd* it, afooar he killed it.

Dandher, literally a blow of such force as to cause shaking; for "dandhers" is a shivering fit; and "dandhering" is trembling. "Ah gav him a left-handed *dandher*, an doon he went."

Dhrissin, (dressing)—a flogging. "Ah'll gi tha a good *dhrissin* doon."

Dhrop, to knock down with the fist. "Behave thisen, or Ah'll *dhrop* tha." (Ice. *drepe*, a blow). Also used to threaten a flogging. "If tha dissn't dhrop it (give up) Ah'll *dhrop* thoo."

Dhrub, to flog. "He'll get weel *dhrubbed*, an sahve him reet."

Differ, a wordy quarrel. "Ah heeahd tell you'd had a *differin boot* (bout); bud, whativver meead ya *differ?*

Dig, to poke with a stick, &c. "He ga' ma a *dig* i' ribs, an its as sare as can be."

Ding or Deng, (Ice. dengja, to hammer) "He *dung* ma

doon." Prof. Skeat (Ety. Dicty.) describes *ding* as a true English strong verb, though not found in A.S. In the York Mystery Plays, 10, 30, we have

> •   "*Dyng* þam doune
>   Tylle all be dede."

Dust, (Ice. dustra, to tilt, fight—Cleasby, Page 109) a scolding, a quarrel or fight. To "kick up a *dust*" is to create a disturbance, while to have your jacket "dusted" is to be well flogged with a stick, leaving not much *dust* in your garments.

Esh, so called from the esh (ash) plant being the instrument used by the castigator.

Feeat, to foot, to kick. "*Feeat* him."

Fell, a knock-down blow. "If tha dissn't mahnd (take care) Ah sall be givin tha a *fell* inoo." (soon).

Fetch, to deliver a blow. "Ah *fetcht* him a crack ower heead, an that sattel'd him."

Fillip, a quick stinging blow.

Fisty Cuffs, a stand-up fight.

Gob-Fight, literally a mouth fight. A wordy quarrel.

Hammer, to flog severely with some instrument. Next tahm he diz it, Ah 'll *hammer* him weel.

Haze, to beat. (Ice. ausa, to abuse or scold. "Linc. and the Danes," p. 336.) Hence "hazing," a beating, a chastisement.

Hezzle, to flog, as with a hezzle (hazel) rod. "If Ah catch tha, mi lad, Ah 'll *hezzle* thi hide fo' tha."

Hiding, a flogging on the *hide*, or back. "Ah 's feeard mi fayther 'll gi ma a good *hidin*."

Hod, a punishment, a flogging. "Ah 'll gi tha sum *hod* afooar lang."

Hum, to beat or flog, also a punishment inflicted by boys on an obstinate player. They lug (pull) his hair, or strike him with their caps, saying "Hum, hum, hum," long drawn out. Such pulling or striking being continued until their

leader cries out "Off!" when all must at once desist, or be
subject to a like punishment themselves.

Jowl, to knock together. " None jangill nor *jolle* at my
gate." York Pl., 307, 14. " Ah'll *jowl* thi heead an wall
tegither."

Knap, (1) a slight blow; (2) to receive punishment.
" Thoo'll *knap* it."

Lam, to beat. (Ice. lemja). " *Lam* intiv him."

Leather, sometimes "lather" (Ice. lauðrungr), so called
from the *leather* strap used for administering punishment.

Leeace, (lace) to flog. " Ah'll *leeace* his jacket for him,
if Ah can catch him."

Let Dhraave, to strike with full force. " He up wiv his
neeaf (fist) an *let dhraave* at him, full slap."

Licks, a chastisement. " Thoo'll get thi *licks*, mi lad, when
thi fayther gets ti knaw." " Ah whop (hope) he weean't *lick*
ma, for his *lickins* hots (hurt) yan."

Linch, a sharp, sudden blow with a pliable instrument.
" He *lincht* ma i' feeace wiv his whip."

Loondher, to abuse, to knock about. " What's tha
loondherin him aboot like that for? What's he deean?"

Lug, to pull hair or ears. The ear itself is called a "lug."

Loonge, a thumping blow.

Lump, to beat on the head with sufficient violence to
cause a lump.

Mell, literally, to *mallet*. (Ice. mölva, to beat). Sometimes
" mill " is used. A mallet is called a mell.

Mob, a punishment among boys, inflicted by striking with
caps, knotted handkerchiefs, &c. On the 29th of May (Royal
Oak Day) any boy who lacked the loyal symbol, a sprig of
oak, would be *mobbed*, *i.e.* pelted with eggs, not always
fresh-laid.

Mump, a blow on the mouth, given with the back of the
hand. " Ah gav him a *mump* ower gob."

Nail, to flog, to beat. "Jack Wilson lad brak oor windher wiv a cobble-steean, an Bob did *nail* him fo 't."

Nevill, to beat with the *neaf* or fist. (Ice. hnefi, the fist).

Nobble, to strike on the nob (head) with a stick. Punch kills Judy by *nobbling* her.

Nope, to strike on the head or knuckles with a stick.

Pick, to push suddenly. "He *pickt* ma doon, just fo' nowt at all, an then thowt betther on 't an *pickt* ma up ageean."

Plug, to strike with the fist. "A good *pluggin* is what thoo desahves."

Quaver, to pretend to strike.

Pooak, to *poke*, or push. Similar to "pick," though *picking* is done by the hand, and *poking* by some instrument.

Pummel, to strike with the fist. "*Pummel* him weel."

Rag, to tease, to aggravate. (Ice. ragja, to slander). "Ah 'll *rag* him weel aboot that lass he 's getten, see if Ah deeant."

Rap, a quick blow.

Rattle, a blow on the head. "A *rattle* ower lug."

Rosselin, literally, a roasting, a good sound beating.

Rumpus, a disturbance, a quarrel.

Sauvin, a flogging, a chastisement.

Scaup, to beat about the *scalp* (head).

Scrag, to seize roughly by the *scrag* of the neck. "Noo, hook it (go away) or Ah 'll *scrag* tha, an mak tha gan.

Scrap, a slight quarrel, *i.e.* only a *scrap* or small piece of a fight. "Oh! bayns only had a *scrap ;* they didn't hot (hurt) yan anuther."

Set teeah, a set to, a regular fight. "There was a regular *set teeah,* i' Back Looan (Lane), ower that cock-fightin job."

Skelp, (Ice. skella, to strike) to strike with the open hand on some fleshy part. "Thoo can gan oot an laik (play), bud if thoo mucks thisen Ah 'll gi tha a good *skelpin.*"

Skin, to flog severely. "Bon tha! Ah'll *skin* tha wick, thoo young rackapelt." (scamp).

Slap, (like skelp), a blow with the open hand.

Slate, to rebuke, abuse (Ice. sletta, to slap, to dab).

Slinge, to strike with a pliable, or supple instrument. "He *slinged* ma wiv a whip."

Slipe, a sharp gliding blow, with the open hand. "Jack gat sike a *slipe* ower gob, that his lips was brussen."

Sloonge, a heavy blow with the open hand. "Thoo'll get a *sloonge* ower heead thareckly."

Slug, (another form of "slog;") to beat with any instrument. "Let's *slug* Tom Smithers, he put saut uppa slittherin-spot." (salt on the sliding-place).

Snape, (Ice. sneypa, to disgrace, &c.) to check. "Ah sud *snape* that bayn, an nut let him hev his awn way iv ivvery thing, like his muther diz."

Sooal, to beat, as with the *sole* of a slipper.

Sowle, to chastise. "He'll go," he says, "and *sowle* the porter of Rome gates by the ears." (Coriolanus, iv., 5).

Spank, to flog, (like slap and skelp). "Be quiet, and give up gennin (whining) or Ah'll *spank* tha."

Sneezer, a violent blow on the nose.

Suff, a blow, or hard knock, sufficient to make one draw in the breath, as when suffering from a spasm of pain.

Swinge, a blow with a whip or any pliable thing. (A.S., swing, a whip, blow).

Swingel, like swinge. (A.S., swinegel, a lash.)

Swipe, like swinge. (Ice. svipa, a whip) From this word we get the diminutive "swipple," the whipping part of a flail.

Switch, a slight blow with a lash, or a thin pliant rod called a *switch*.

Tannin, a beating on the back, like "hidin."

Tew, a struggle. "We had a teeafish *tew*, an Ah sweeat like a brock wi' *tewin* seeah."

Thresh, literally to beat with a flail.

Throonce, to bustle about, to drive off.

Thropple, to seize by the throat, or *thropple.*

Thump, to strike heavily on the back.

Tift, *a* tiff, a slight quarrel.

Twenk, to lash with a whip or pliant rod.

Twilt, to flog with some instrument. " *Twilt* his jacket for him, a pawky young raskil." "He desahves a good *twiltin.*"

Wale, to beat with a stick sufficiently hard to make " wales," hence " wallopin," a severe flogging. .

Wappin, a flogging. " Thoo'll get thi *waps.*"

Welting, chastisement by means of a " welt," a leather strap. A welt is sewn on to a boot upper, and the sole is sewn to the welt.

Whack, to beat. " Ah'll *whack* thi hide for tha, if tha dissn't mahnd."

Whissle, a box on the ears.

Whipe, a stinging, sliding blow, like slipe. " A *whipe* ower heead, or ower lugs."

Yark, to strike with a stick or whip.

Yether, to flog with a yether, a long supple rod used in making a dead fence. When cutting thorns, a hedger will say " If that weean't mak a steeak, it 'll mak a *yether.*" A long discoloured stripe caused by a blow is called a yether.

Yenk, to lash with the extreme end of a whip.

Yuck, to chastise. " He gat his *yucks.*"

A peculiarity of these words is, that many of them are also in common use as adjectives, denoting superlative greatness, or extraordinary fineness. The word retains the same meaning, but the figure is changed from warlike strife to the strife of competition and comparison. Thus we say " a *clinkin* big egg," which means that particular egg will *beat* all others in comparison or competition ; or " a *nailin* stooary," " a *slappin* hoss," " a *sluggin* knife," " a *spankin* meear," (mare) " a *switchin* ton oot," (turn out) " a *thumpin*

big lass," " a *wallopin* big pig," "a *whackin* lie," a *wappin*
score, (at cricket) &c.

Some of these adjectives are used as nouns; thus, "That 's
a whacker," means that particular article surpasses all others
of the same kind.   So "thumper," "cracker," "nailer,"
"nobbler," "plugger," "rattler," "skelper," "slapper,"
"slugger," "spanker," &c., are articles of superior or superlative quality.

CHAPTER IV.

SPECIMENS OF THE DIALECT.

A STOOARY O' BONNICK BOGGLE.

(Bonnick—Bonwick, near Skipsea. There is now no village,
as there once was ; only traces of foundations round Joan's
Dyke, which formed the village pond. Daffodils grow
wild in one field, which formed the flower gardens of the
departed cottages. One farmhouse, High Bonwick, and
another, Low Bonwick, are the only two houses in the
township. The Cawsey is the causeway, or raised road from
Skipsea to Skipsea Brough, across the marsh now drained
by the White Marr Drain).

Aye, what a do we had oot o' Billy Swaby an his malak
wi' Bonnick boggle. Billy had been at Rooaze and Croon,
wheear they'd been jawin aboot bahgeist an ghooast stooaries,
whahl he sed he dozen't gan heeam. Hooivver, oot he had
ti gan at last, an as he shaffled on Cawsey, he lewkt aboot
him, fost o' yah sahd an then o' tudher, an ommast dodhered
hissen ti bits, when a awd coo beealed ower hedge at him,
great bawmy 'at he is ! Whah, bon it ! he's that soft he mun
be a bohn feeal !

Tonnin looan end ti Bonnick, beughs o' big esh three, at

,cooaner, meead it as dahk as pick, an he skoothered alang
hedge sahd like a patthridge fo' fear White Lady sud cum
wivoot her heead; or bahgeist, wiv ees as big as teeah saucers.

Nowt com, an he went on whahl he com inti slack, just
afooar ya get ti Lo Bonnick, wheear rooad was all blathery,
an he cudn't find yat, bud went splawthering aboot, fost inti
hedge an then inti dike, an i' end, gat ower palins, sweearin
at boggle had teean yat away.

He gat on ti rooad ageean, efther ommast tumlin inti
Jooan Dike, an hadn't geean monny sthrahds afooar he fell
ower summat i' middle o' rooad, at was soft an hairy; an
what jumped up an blared at him as he scrawmed an
rawmed aboot i' muck. Poor Billy was ommast flaid oot
ov his wits, an thowt he was getten, bud when he fan his
legs, he peg-legged away full pelt; an tell'd fooaks at he'd
tummeled ower Bonnick Boggle; bud it was only Fahmer
Stork white fuzzack at was laid i' middle o' rooad, as sike
fond things offense diz.

HOO NEDDY KIRBY WAS ROBBED.

Neddy was a teealer, an used ti gan oot ti wahk, yan or
mare days at a tahm. He'd had a job at Black Bull, for
aboot fower days, an efther hevin two or three good sups o'
ther yal set off ti walk heeam. Neet was dahk, bud Neddy knew
rooad, an set off whislin, wiv his geeas on his sleeve-booad,
slung ower his shooldher. Gainist rooad heeam was doon
bi Fahmer Gibson plantin; an as Neddy was shaflin on, bi
sahd o' plantin, a jenny oolat skreeaked oot, an freetened
him ommast oot ov his wits. Off he set, as hahd as ivver
his bowdy-kite legs wad carry him; an, as neet was pick
dahk, he cudn't see wheear he was gannin, an tummelled

ç

ower a pissimire hill, an his geeas hit him a cloot ower back
ov his heead. He thowt robbers was on him, an rooared for
pity ; tewk all brass oot ov his pockets, laid it uppo grund,
an set off ageean ; an nivver stopt whahl he gat heeam, and
telled em he'd been robbed. Sum fooaks went on next
mooanin, an fan all Neddy brass uppo grund, just wheear
he'd left it. They gat it all up, an then axt Ned an a lot
mare ti gan ti Black Oss, and let Ned tell his stooary, whahl
they steead threeat all roond/ When all munny was spent,
they tell'd Ned wheeas munny had bowt yal, an sum on em
yit say they wish Neddy Kirby was robbed ageean. And
Neddy his-sen gat seeah mad ower it, that lads can awlas get
his rag oot wi shooting up passidge " Wheah robbed Neddy?"

A EEAST YORKSHER STOOARY.

Ah say, Jim ! hez tha heea'd tell what a dooment Navvy
Bob had wi' that deead chap, at they gat oot ov oor scawdin
tub? Thoo knaws, chap dhroondid his-sen i' tub ; an he'd
stiffen'd all ov a heeap, seeah at they couldn't mak a deeacent
coffin for him. They rigg'd up a sthrang teeable iv oor bahn,
an stuck him on it. They gat yah booad across his knees
wiv a lot o' fower steean weights on it, an a lot mare uppov
another booad, across his kist, ti sthreyten him a bit. Sum
ov oor lads ment hevin a spree oot o' Bob ; seeah aboot nahn
o'clock they oppen'd bahn deear, an threw a cat an dog in,
tahd tegither. They fowt, an spit, an scratid, an growl'd,
an meead sike a row iv hooal, that Bob gat up offa creeal,
wheear he'd been liggin, an gat a hedgin-steeak, ti hammer
em oot ageean. The things fullockt aboot bahn fleear,
undher teeable an atwixt thrussle legs, ower secks o' wheeat,
an ommast throppled thersens ower hales ov a hickin-barra,

at was fast amang secks. They swither'd aboot like mad things. Bob efther em, wi steeak iv his hand, cossin an sweearin, an sayin they wer divvel his-sen. Enoo, they ran atwixt his legs, an knocked him ageean booad across deead chap kist, an knockt it off, whahl weights tummel'd doon wiv a clatter, and deead chap sprang bolt upreet, as sthreet as a dart. Bob ton'd roond, when he heead row, for he thowt he'd knockt teeable an all ower; an when he saw deead chap sittin up, he tewk steeak i' beeath hans, swung it ower his heead, an sed "Thoo lig thi-sen doon ageean; Ah can sattle a dog and cat wivoot thah help."

What com next Ah deean't knaw; for oor lads skoother'd off, fo' fear Bob sud hear em laffin.

Next mooanin Bob wadn't speeak a wod o' what had happened; bud he'd manidged ti sup all yal an smewk all bacca they'd gin him; an pleeace was all ov a reek like a lahm kill, ommast all next day.

PAHSON AN KEEAL POT.

(Keeal pot—kail pot, *i.e.*, cabbage pot, or broth pot. A spherical cast iron vessel, of two or three gallons capacity, having three feet to ensure safe standing. It has two small lugs (ears) to which the semi-circular handle is fastened).

Oor pahson liked owt at was cheeap, an seeah, yah day, he was at a toon, two or three mahls frev heeam, an as he was gannin doon yan o' sthreets, he saw a fellow stanin atop ov a teeable, sellin keeal pots, pooakers, oddments, an kelther-ment. It com intiv his heead at his wife said ti yan o' lasses, afoor he stahted, at they sadly wanted a keeal pot, an seeah he thowt he wad thry ti hev a cheeap bahgan ti tak

heeam wiv him. Just as he went up ti fella, a widda woman
was biddin yan an nahnpence fo' just sike a keeal pot as he
wanted ; an seeah he bad, an sheeah bad, an he bad ageean,
an sheeah bad ageean, an seeah they bad yan ageean tudher,
pahson an widda, for a lang whahl, an iv end, it was knocked
doon ti pahson fo' three an tuppence. Efther paying fo't,
he set off heeam as fast as he could pelt, ti show his awd
deeam what a cheeap bahgan he'd getten, an tell her hoo
he'd bested poor widda. He fost hugged it i' ya hand an then
i' tudher; for it was neeah leet weight, Ah can tell ya.
Efther gannin this gate for aboot a mahl an a hawf or seeah,
he began ti feel tired, an his ayms began ti wahk, whahl he
cud hardlins bahd, an he began ti rue at he'd bowt it. Bud
thowt popt intiv his heead at "A change is as good as a
rist ;" seeah he tewk off his hat and put keeal pot on iv it
pleeace, wiv holla sahd doonwads ti keep it on. Away he
cut across clooases, seeah as neeah-body mud see him huggin
it heeam, fo' fear they sud mak gam on him ; bud afooar he
gat heeam, he had a wahdish beck ti cross ; an as ther was
neeah brig, or owt o' sooat, he was fooact ti lowp ower it.
Seeah he tewk a good lang run, and ower he went like a
steg ; bud when he let at tudher sahd, keeal pot went reet
doon on his heead ower his ees, wiv hannle undher his chin
like lastic. Poor pahson was i' sike a stew. He thried ti
get it off, and thried ageean an ageean, bud he couldn't stor
it a bit—it was as fast as athof it had grown theear. Hoo ti
get heeam he didn't knaw, for he could see nowt, his ees
was reet blocked up. Hawivver, be went on grapin aboot
as weel as he cud, an when he fan yat, he thried ti get thruf,
bud theear he stuck fast, wi keeal pot heead and hannle
through yat bars ; an deeah what he wad he cudn't get lowse,
bud stuck theear for a hoor, botherin and sweeatin like a pig
iv a muck middin, whahl he was all ov a muck lather. It
seeah happened at a man called Bobby Brushwood was
cumin that rooad, an seein summat fast i' yat he meead up

tiv it. When he gat theear he knew it was pahson bi shap
of his legs; an he sed "Maisther, maisther, whativver are
ya deeahin theear? Laws o' me! what a pickle yu'r in!" "Ay,
Bobby!" says pahson, "An is that thoo? Ah's varry glad
thoo's cum'd! Wheear is Ah? What a misfottan this is!"
"Whah, maisther," says Bobby, "hoo's this? Can't ya get
keeal pot offa yer heead?" "Neeah, Bobby, mah lad; it's fast
aneeaf. Ah can't stor it; an Ah's flaid it'll nivver cum off
ageean. Tak hod o' mi hand an leed ma heeam." "Seeah
Ah will, maisther; bud its a varry bad job, 'cos, yu see, yu'll
nivver preeach ni mare tiv uz, wi' that thing atop o' yer
heead." Pahson sed nowt ti this, bud gav a grooan.

Noo, when they gat ti Toon Gate bains com runnin iv all
mandhers o' ways ti see what this thing was at Bobby had
getten, bud neean on em could tell. Sum on em said yan tiv
anuther, "Sitha! sitha! Bobby's getten a young elephant."
"Nay, it isn't; he's catcht a see sahpent." Uthers sed it was
a Greenland beear, or summat like it. Pahson sed nowt
tiv em, thof he heead all they sed.

When he gat heeam there was a do. All docthers roond
aboot was sent for, but they cud deeah neeah gud, nut yan
on em, wivoot they cut his heead off. They pulled an they
screwed, an pahson thried ti back oot his heead, an sluf it
off, bud it was all neeah use; for, deeah what they wad, awd
keeal pot wadn't leeave pahson heead.

At last Bobby says, "Ah've fun oot noo, hoo it'll he' ti
be deean. Let's gan ti blacksmith shop." An away they
all went, riddy aneeaf, especially pahson, at wad he' deean
onny mottal thing ti get keeal pot offan his heead.

When they all gat inti shop, Bobby says, "Noo, maisther,
lig yer heead doon uppa stiddy;" an he ligged it doon uppa
stiddy that varry minnit. Blacksmith then tewk yan o'
biggest hammers he had, an brak keeal pot intiv a thoosan
bits.

Mah wod, bud pahson lewkt rare an glad when he saw

day-leet ageean; an he cut off heeam as fast as he cud,
hoddin beeath hands tiv his lugs; pleeased aneeaf, Ah'll
asseer ya, at he'd getten his heead oot o' that keeal pot.

•   (The Excelsior Reciter p. 248.   Altered)

RIDING THE STANG.

The biggest norrayshun at ivver was seen,
Was yah Collop Munda, on Thistleton Green,
When young Sammy Spadger had wallop'd his wife,
An leeac'd her wivin hawf a inch ov her life.
               When news gat aboot,
               All lads they com oot,
An they raised sike a hullaballo an a shoot,
Sike a beeall an a clatther, a yowp an a yell,
You'd he' swoan at Awd Nick had bont Bible i' hell.
'Cawse Bessy, his wife, thof i' nowt bud print goons,
Was heppenest woman you'd finnd i' ten toons;
Sike a click iv her back, an sa jannack an tall,
An highly beliked an rispected bi all.
Seeah they all on em swore wiv a dash an a dang,
They would get on a stee an would ride him a stang.
               There was Billy Magee,
               Wiv a kest iv his ee,
An a rooas pinned i' frunt ov his best seckaree;
               An young Jabod Rees,
               Skymin oot ov his ees;
               An young Randy Todd,
At wore iv his billy the wing ov a bod;
               An Speelywag Robby,
               The son o' the Bobby;

An Bandy-legged Dick,
Wheeah's fayther was deead, tho' his muther was wick;
An Ellery Crisp,
That had teed up his slops wiv a lang wot-sthreea wisp;
An Goffeny Mile,
Wiv a hat on his heead like a whemmel'd-doon sile;
An young Buckie Sykes,
That was sookin away at a pipe iv his wikes;
An awd Cockie Sharrah,
Wiv a pair ov octoavers as big as a barra;
An lots on em mooar;
There wadn't be yan on em less then two scooar.
Seeah, wi sang an wi' sup,
At "Bull an Blew Munkey" they meead it all up;
An efther some caffle, conthrahviñ, an talkin,
They varry seean manidged ti mak up a mawkin.
Then they borra'd a stee
Fre Billy Magee,
An set beeath mawkin an Billy asthrahd;
'Cawse his voice was sa rough, an his mooth was sa wahd.
O lawk! 'twas a whopper,
Like top ov a hopper,
An they knew he cud let oot the poethry propper.
Then they hugged him roond toon,
Bi the leet o' the moon,
An all the awd tosspots wer efther em soon,
Some wivoot onny hats, an wivoot onny shoon,
'Cawse sthreets they wer dhry
As a barley-meeal pie.
There was young lads an lasses, an awd wives an dames,
Wi ther cassimere approns belapt roond ther aymes,
An awd Dawcy Rowlytubs ran inti sthreet,
Wiv a shaff o' spice-breead sha'd just getten ti eeat,
'Cawse sha said at sha wadn't be slowpt ov her meeat.

Seeah sha chowed as sha ran,
Ti keep up wiv awd man,
Puffing like a steeam booat,
An varry nigh slockened wi crums doon wrang throoat,
An sha just gat ti chotch deer (the yan they call sooth),
When they tooted the hawboy, an Billy ga mooth.

" Here we cum wi' the soond o' the hohn,
Been betther for this woman if this man had nivver been
    bohn.
Here we cum wiv a ran-a-dan-dan,
It's neeather fo' your cause nor mah cause at Ah ride this
    stang,
But for Sammy, the butcher, his wife he did bang;
He banged her, he banged her, he banged her indeed,
He banged her, poor creeathur, afoor sha stood need;
He tewk neeather stick, staff, iron, nor stower,
Bud he up wiv his neeaf, an knockt her ower;
Up-stairs a-back o' bed,
Sike a riot as nivver was led.
Doon stairs aback o' door,
He banged her whahle her back was sooar.
Poor thing was se scared that she ran wiv a fullock,
And wi' cowlrake he then knockt her doon like a bullock.
Sha oppened her gob, and sha let oot a yowp,
And he bazzacked her whahl she was stiff as a stowp.
He gev her a woncer, a twicer, an a back-hander,
'Twas a sin an a sham, was the way at he tanned her.
Noo, all you good people, wo live i' this raw,
We'd he' ya tak nooatis, for this is oor law—
If onny o' you husbands your good wives you do bang,
We'll get on this stee, and we'll ride you a stang."
As seean as he finisht they set up a cheer,
An Jabod collected sum coppers fo' beer,

Whahl all the awd gossaps began fo' ti jabber
As hahd as ther tungs could be liggin ti labber.
They called Sammy Spadger a bulletowst hog,
A shitwig at 's just fit ti live iv a bog,
A muckflee ti gi' tiv a tooad or a frog,
They called him all neeames fre dival ti dog.
   " Aye !" said Sally Magee,
   " He sud just hev had me !
   Ah 'd ha' meeade him pay dear !
   Ah 'd ha' gi'n him what cheer !
Ah 'd ha' gi'n him bell-tinker an paddy-whack sauce.
Ah 'd ha' gi'n him a teeast o' Nan Clappison's dose.
Wi yan o' them there ! Ah 'd ha' knockt him doon stoddy,
An riven his liver-pin oot ov his body."
An Sally, she browt doon her fist wiv a soss
At wad sahtenly brokken the back ov a hoss.
Seeah they kept on a cheerin, an shootin, an talkin,
As they went roond the villidge an followed the mawkin.
   An Billy Magee,
   At was set uppa stee,
   He reeled oot the rahms,
An Ah 'll sweear at he reeled em oot full fifty tahms.
   Three neets did they hod
This blissid norrayshun, an then on the thod,
They 'd a booanfire, an beer, an sike capers an games,
An they hung Sammy Spadger, his mawkin, i' flames,
Wi crackers all teed tiv his legs an his aymes,
   An sike 'n a spree
   As you nivver did see,
An varry fow fooaks gat ti bed awhahl three.
'Twas the biggest norrayshun at ivver was seen,
When they bont Sammy Spadger on Thisselton Green.

                    Geo. Lancaster.

A NEET OV HORROR.

A THREW STOOARY.

Noo monny a day sin, as Ah've heead tell,
A horrubble neet ti John Smith yance befell.
Iv a Howdherness villidge he'd lived all his days,
An been stiddy as clock-wahk iv all his good ways.
A hahd-wahkin man John had been all his life,
An had a good helper i' Nanny—his wife.
Bud Nanny, lang sin, had geean tiv her rist,
An her sperit had sooar'd up ti "realms o' the blist."
Ther banes had grown up, getten married, an geean,
An awd man was left, wiv his-sen, all aleean.

Bi meeans of his thrade, an a wee bit o' grund,
He'd manidged ti cog up aboon fotty pund.
He'd monny a anksome lewk at his store,
Noo carefully hed iv a newk ov a dhrawer.

Awd fooaks deean't sleep soond, and John wad oft keep
Awakken for hoors, nut venthrin ti sleep,
Fa fear at sum theeaves—sum law rubbishly thrash,
Wad brake intiv his hoose an walk off wiv his cash.

Yah dahk winther neet, as he laid, full o' fear,
He fancied he heead theeaves at his back deear.
He lissen'd—O dear! Seer as fate they we' there;
An his honest awd heart noo felt pangs o' dispair.
Bud he seean gat a leet, an then doon stairs he went;
O' defendin his threasure he was fully bent.
Ti boak all sike chaps o' ther vahl theeavish fun,
He'd wahsly pavahded his-sen wiv a gun.

He darkt asahde deear, an then, wivoot doot,
He heead what vahl wretches ootsahde wer aboot.
His hoose steead apayte, seeah ni help cud he get,
Ti defend him ageean sike a vagabond set.

He spok em, bud nivver a wod did they say,
Bud at his awd deear kept scrubbin away ;—
Seeam'd thryin ti find sum wake spot or sum crack,
Ti put in a gavlack an fooace his deear back.
He tell'd em, hey, ower an ower ageean,
If they didn't give ower, at he'd varry seean
Fire off his gun at em, then they'd repent day
At ther theeavish dezahns had led em that way.
It seeam'd at they thowt at he hadn't a gun,
An at fing'rin his gold wad be far betther fun .
Then runnin away, like cawf-hearted chickins,
An missin ther chance o' sike golden pickins.
They laboured si hahd—went at it sa bold,
John saw they'd detahmin'd o' hevvin his gold.

All threeats an all wahnins alike preeav'd i' vain,
Fo' theeaves seeam'd detahmin'd his threasure ti gain.
Wiv his gun riddy raised, he steead beyont deear ;
Nowt bud firin' wad seeave him, he felt varry seear.

A pull at gun thricker, an slap-bang went ball,
An in flew awd deear an deear-steead an'all :
Like a leetnin-flash, in it flew iv a crack,
An knockt poor awd Smith uppa fleear ov his back.

Things noo tewk a ton ; an Smith, nut si bold,
Thowt mare ov his-sen, an less ov his gold ;
An dhreeadin a moddherous endin ti sthrife,
Cried "Oh! tak mi munney—fo' God seeak spare mi life"
O' massy his heart noo wad ommost dispair ;
Bud his cries we' ni use—ther was neeabody there.
Smith laid uppa fleear, wi' brokken deear on him,
Expectin at yance at theeaves wad be on him.
Wi fear an thrimlin be was quiet oot o' breeath ;
Bud, beeath insahde an oot, all was still as grim deeath.
"Hoo is this," he thowt tiv his-sen, as he laid,
"When they've smasht in mi deear at they've gin up
    ther thrade ?"

Bud still he felt seear at, wiv all ther pains
Ti get in, they'd cum back, an secure ther gains.
 Efther liggin a bit, as neeah yan com near,
Smith venthered ti crowl frev undher his deear,
An lewkt oot inti dahk an cawd midneet air,
Bud nivver a soul nor a soond was ther there.

All throo that dahk neet he sat shiv'rin wi fear,
Feelin sahtan at theeaves wad be lurkin near,
An seean wad be cumin, ther booty ti gain,
An seeah past his neet, i' terror an pain.

At last mooanin dawned, ti Smith greeat releeaf,
An villidge seean heead ov his horror an greeaf :
Like wahld-fire it ran—ivvery hoose iv eeach sthreet
Noo rang wi sad news o' John horrubble neet.

Leeather on, threwth o' matther com sthrangely oot,
An fooaks saw at yance what all row was aboot :—
Bob Johnson had cum'd tiv a despad loss—
Sumbody or uther had shutten his hoss.
Bob hoss, i' neet tahm, hevvin all his awn way,
Felt a lahtle inclahn'd ower fences ti sthray :
Smith gahdin was next ti Bob field, an his fence
Was awful an bad, an seeah, it seeams, thence
Bob hoss, nut wi views o' reet varry clear,
Sthrade ower awd fence an up ti Smith deear ;
An, findin deear was a conveeaniant spot,
Began imitatin weel-knawn loosy Scot,
Bi rubbin his flanks an his sahds, i' grand stahle,
Bud mebby he fail'd ti "Bless Duke ov Argahle."

Smith wahnins an threeats ti Bob hoss we' ni use,
An he mud as weel he' been still as a moose ;
Bud his bullit was mare then hoss feelins cud beear,
Seeah he up wiv his heels an smasht in Smith deear.

T. HOLDERNESS.

APRIL FEEAL DAY.

Showin hoo Matty Muckspoot went ti fetch a storrup-oil
freezin-machine.

What a feeal is oor Jack!
⠀Ah seear he wad mak
Onnybody gan ranty, he hez sike daft ways ;
An if he dizn't olther he 'll shooaten mah days.
⠀⠀He 's sike a greeat fowt
⠀・⠀At he thinks aboot nowt
Bud makkin all mischief at ivver he can :
He 's mare like a skeeal-lad, a deal, then a man.
Last Munda (All Feeal Day) he cudn't let pass
Bud what he mud mak a greeat feeal ov oor lass.
⠀⠀" Here, Matty ! " sez he,
Ah wish thoo wad just gan doon villidge fo' me,
An ax Tommy Smootins, wheah lives clooase bi Green,
Ti send ma his storrup-oil freezin machine."

⠀⠀Just then Matty was fillin
Sum sausingers oot o' sum pigs they 'd been killin :
Bud Ah 'll say this for Matty—sha 's civil an willin.
⠀⠀Seeah sha weshes her neeaves,
⠀⠀An slipes doon her sleeaves,
An thraws a reead ton-ower atop ov her sahk,
An gans off i' height ov her thrang an her wahk.
An when sha gat there sha fan Tommy at yam,
An, ov cooas, Ah deean't doot, he was weel up ti gam.
⠀⠀Seeah he gans inti byre,
An fills a awd ken wi sum wheels an sum wire,
An sum seeaves, an a krewk offa feyin-machine,
An a lot o' sike kelther as nivver was seen,

He sez, "Matty, it lewks i' bad oather, Ah seear,
Bud tell him it hezzn't been used o' fahve year;
  An it wants a good boilin
  Afooar he puts oil in."

Seeah Matty, sha gans, luggin it off doon toon sthreets;
An ivvery yan goffnin an gooavin sha meets:
  An sha thowt it was queear,
  At fooaks gooaved oot o' deear:
Bud sha thowt it was all lang o' nut beein dhrist;
An it sagged her poor aymes seeah she had it ti rist.
  Seeah, whahl sha was pantin,
  Up cums Billy Bantin,—
It mebby mud be twenty minnits past ten aboot,—
Sez he, "Matty, what for is tha luggin awd ken aboot?"
  "Awd ken!" sez oor Matty;
"It's a storrup-oil freezin-machine, thoo daft watty!"
  "Whah," sez he, "thoo greeat stoavy!
  Thoo goffeny goavy,
  It's thoo at's daft watty!
Jack's makkin a greeat April Feeal o' tha, Matty!"

  Noo, sha was iv a puckerin!
Ti think at oor Jack sud sa shamfully suck her in.
  Sha banged awd ken doon,
  Reet i' middle o' toon,
An com skelpin yam, as thof summat had bont her,
Or thoosans o' rattens an mice was behont her.
  Lawk! hoo sha did rooar,
  For meeast ov a hooar!
  Whah, it was ower bad;
  An Ah felt buggy mad,
Ti think at oor ottherpooak clunch ov a ass
Sud mak sike a April-daft watty o' lass.

Sha sweears at sha'll give him as good as he sent,
If sha hez ti think ower it up ti next Lent.
Sha taks it ti haht, yu knaw,—Ah sud, mi-sen;
An sha's been iv a mullygrubs ivver sin then.

GEO. LANCASTER.

PART OF THE FIRST CHAPTER OF GENESIS, IN THE NORTH
HOLDERNESS DIALECT, SHOWING, MORE PARTICULARLY, THE
OMISSION OF THE DEFINITE ARTICLE:

1. I' beginnin' God meead heaven an' ath oot o' nowt.
2. An' ath was wi'oot shap, an' emty: and dahkness was
uppa feeace o' deep. An' sperit o' God storred uppa feeace
o' watthers.
3. An' God sed, Let ther' be leet: an' ther' was leet.
4. An' God seed leet, at it was good: an' God devahded
leet fre' dahkness.
5. An' God call'd leet Day, an' dahkness he call'd Neet.
An' neet an' mooanin' we' fost day.
6. An' God sed, Let ther be a fahmament i' midst o'
watthers, an' let it devahde watthers fre' watthers.
7. An' God meead fahmament, an' devahded watthers
'at wer' undher fahmament fre' watthers 'at were aboon
fahmament, an' it was seeah.
8. An' God call'd fahmament Heaven. An' neet an'
mooanin' we' second day.
9. An' God sed, Let watthers 'at's undher heaven be
gether'd tegither inti' yah pleeace, an' let dhry land appear;
an' it was seeah.
10. An' God call'd dhry land Ath: an' getherin' tegither
o' watthers he call'd Seeas: an' God seed 'at it was good.

11.   An' God sed, Let ath bring fooath gess, yahb yieldin' seed, an' frewt three yieldin' frewt efther his kahnd, wheease seed is iv itsen, uppa yath : an' it was seeah.

12.   An' ath browt fooath gess, an' yahb yieldin' seed efther his kahnd, an' three yieldin' frewt, wheease seed was iv itsen, efther his kahnd : an' God seed 'at it was good.

13.   An' neet an' mooanin' we' thod day.

14.   An' God sed, Let ther' be leets i' fahmament o' heaven ti devahde day fre neet : an' let 'em be fa sahns, an' fa seeahsons, an' fa days, an' yeeahs.

15.   An' let 'em be fa leets i' fahmament o' heaven ti gi' leet uppa yath : an' it was seeah.

———

Note.—In the Authorised Version the definite article is used 52 times in these 15 verses.

(Holderness Glossary, p. 18.)

CHAPTER VI.

ILLUSTRATED AND ILLUSTRATIVE GLOSSARY.

Aboon, above. "Nay, bayn, that's *aboon* me," said a mother to her child, who had asked a question the mother could not answer.

"*Abowne* it sall I be." York Pl., 4, 87.

"This is the name þat es *abowne* all names." Pr. Tr., 1.

Aback-o-beyont, behind; behind-hand; out of the way.

"That slaw beggar's awlas *aback-o-beyont* wiv his wahk." H. G.

" Ah 'll send tha *aback-o-beyont,* wheear craws its (eats) hawpnies." H. G.

Addle, to earn.

" Ah aint *addled* saut (salt) ti mi taties this mawnin." H. G.

"Short harvests make short *addlings.*" Eng. Prov., p. 349.

Admire, to observe; to notice with astonishment.

"An when Ah gat there; oh, this Ah did *admeyr,*
Ti see so monny lusty lads, asitting roond the fire." H. G.

Ageean, near to; against.

"He tummel'd *ageean* bucket, an cut his heead."

"And lith (lies) *aȝein* þe lawe." P. P., III, 155.

ᴅ

Ageeat, engaged on ; begun. (Literally, on gate. See " Gate.")

" He 's *ageeat* ov a theeakin (thatching) job."

" Let 's get *ageeat* on 't."

Akest, crooked ; warped ; twisted. (Literally on cast, *i.e.,* cast on one side). A person who squints is said to have a *kest* in the eye.

"It 's all *akest.*"

Ake, to wander about aimlessly and idly.

" He was *akin* aboot all day lang ; an all fo nowt." H. G.

In Lincolnshire, an idle worthless fellow is termed a " *hakes.*" L. and D.

Anenst, against ; next ; near to ; with.

"It was ower *anenst* floor-mill."

" But *anentis* God all thinges ben possible." Wic., Matt., 19, 26.

Arr, (Ice., arr and örr,) a scar.

" He 's badly pock-*arr'd* (pock-marked)."

" Myn *erres* (scars, wounds), rotid." Psalter, 37, 5.

Arse, the back part of anything. The *arse* of a cart, or a plough.

Atheril, a shapeless mass. Literally a mass of poisonous matter ; from A.-S., ater—poison. From this word comes attercop (a spider), literally, the poison-bag.

" Poor fellow ! he was smasht all tiv (to) a *atheril.*" H.G.

Axe, to ask. (A. S., acsian, to ask.)

"I may namore *axe.*" P.P., IV., 102.

"Go ye, and *axe* ye." Wic., Matt., 2, 8.

Backer-end—the farther end of a room.

" Y'u cudn't see ti *backer-end* o' spot, it was seeah full o' reek."

Bahgeeast, A ghost-bear ; a bug-bear ; that which causes fear or terror. A little active wilful fellow, who filled his mother with fear and terror, by constantly running away from her, was addressed thus, " Cum here, thoo lahtle *bagheeast*; thoo ommast flays (affrights) ma oot o' mi wits."

Balk, (1) (Ice., bálkr) a transverse beam ; a beam. "A fower-hoss *balk.*"

> "For that *balke* will no man vs blame
> To cut it for the kyng." York Pl., 339, 68.

(2) A strip or ridge, forming a land-boundary.

"Have an eye to the heades and *balkes.*" Best, p. 28.

"Dikeres and delueres digged up the *balkes.*" P.P., VI, 109.

(3) A grassy headland in a ploughed field.

(4) A grasy lane or road.

(5) To shirk, or leave undone.

"They. ....*balk* the right way, and strayen abroad." Sh. Cal., (Sept).

(6) To shrink from. "Awd meear *balkt* at yat stowp."

(7) To turn, with loathing, from food or drink, so as nearly to vomit.

"Ah ommast *balkt* mi heart up."

Ballocks, testicles. Literally, little balls.

"Taken away the *ballokes.*" Wic., Lev., 22, 24.

Band, string ; rope.

> "A moder ass yee sal þar find,
> And ye hir sal vndo,
> Vte of hir *band.*" Curs. Mun. 14,969.

Baste, A tailor's and dress-maker's term, meaning to tack or sew slightly. A tacking thread is a *basting*-thread.

> "And on her legs, she painted buskins wore,
> *Basted* with bends of gold." F.Q., 5, 5, 3.

Bate, to reduce in cost ; to abate.

"His wife is more costly, and he *bates* her in tires" (dress). Micro.

Bayns, bairns ; children.

> "For Marie, love of heuene,
> þat bar þat blisful *barne.*" P. P., II., 2.

"Q ! *barnes*, it waxes clere." York Pl., 51, 183,

Beald, a shelter for cattle ; any shelter.

"Noo, lads, let's gan ti *beal* sahd ov hedge.".

Beeal, to shout out ; to cry ; to bellow.   Akin to *bawl.*

"Ah was ommast flay'd oot o' mi wits, when awd bull *beeal'd* oot at ma."

Besom, a birch broom.

"Clensed with *besyms.*"   Wic., Matt., 12, 45.

Besom Bet is the name of the personator of a female in the "Fond Pleeaf Procession," on Plough Monday.   Besomheead is a term of contempt for one with little mental capacity.

Beck, (Ice. bekkr ; Swed. bäck ; Dan. bæk ; Du. beek ; Ger. bach), a stream ; a brook.

This is the common name for streams, though some are worthy, notably the trout-streams at Driffield, of being called rivers.   Beyond this generic name, they are all nameless, except when the name of the adjacent village is added or prefixed for the sake of distinction.

"Thou brast welles and *beckis.*"   Psalter, 73, 16.

"The watirs ran, and the *beckis* bolnyd" (swelled).   Psalter, 73, 23.

Beldher, to blubber and cry.

"Ah nivver heead sike a *beldherin* bayn i' all mah booan days."   H. G.

Belly-wahk, stomach-ache ; colic.

"Sick of the idle crick, and the *belly-wahk* in the heel." Eng. Prov., 349. (See wahk—pain).

Bent, determined ; obstinately inclined.

"Let him gan his awn way ! He's *bent* o' deeahin wrang."

"Thou art *bent* to die alone."   Spenser's Daphnaïda, 141.

Beugh, a bough.

"The *bughes* are the armes with the handes." Pr. of Con., 680.

Bolt, an arrow.   Now obsolete.   See Similes p. 21.

"I bent my *bolt* against the bush."   Sh. Cal. (March).

Boult, to sift. Obsolete.

Saying, "He now had *boulted* all the floure." F.Q. 2, 4, 24.

Bile, (A.-S., byl; Du., buil; Ice., bola) a boil.

"The *byil* of Egypt." Wic., Deut., 28, 27.

"Bayn's getten a *bile* on his aym (arm) an can't cum ti skeeal."

Bink, a bench; a bank. (A.-S., benc; Du. bank; Icel. bekkr; Swed. and Dan. bänk).

"And gret on him full tendirli,
And þan on *bink* he sitt him bi." Curs. Mun., 50, 57.

"And I schall buske to þe *benke*,
Wher baners are bright." York Pl., 227, 188.

The rocky ledges at the mouth of the Humber are called Stoney *Binks*; and a ledge of chalk, at Flambrough Head, is named Stottle *Binks*.

Black and **Blew**, discoloured.

"Poor bayne had been hammered seeah mich, at it was all *black an' blew*."

"þe son wex *blak and bloo*." Curs. Mun. 958.

Blash, weak, poor stuff.

It was a public tea, and one woman said to another, "We've had tweea sooats o' *blash* ti-neet—fost *blashy* teea, an then *blashy* talk."

Blathery, wet and muddy.

"Ah've getten *blather'd* up ti mi een, rooads was sa *blathery*."

"*Batter*" is known as "*blatther*"; and a batter-pudding as a "*blatther-puddin*".

Bluther, to cry. A form of "blubber."

"Noo then! let's he' nooah mair o' that *blutherin* an beeahn."

"Her faire face with teares was fowly *blubberin*." F.Q., 2, 1, 13.

Boggle, an apparition. Derived from "*bug*." See "bahgeeast." In the West Riding the word becomes "boggard."

"Ghastly *bug* does greatly them affeare." F.Q., 2, 3, 20.

Bole, the enlarged, round (literally, swollen) part.

This word is nearly obsolete, and is restricted to two objects—the hand, and the body or trunk of a tree. The palm of the hand is known as the *bole* of the hand. Akin to ball, bowl, boil (round tumour), bulge, and bag.

"For *bollyng* (swelling) of her wombe." P.P., vi., 218

"þe king (Pharaoh) herd þis and weped sare,
    And sagh (saw) men's bodis *bolnud* (swollen) ware."
    Curs. Mun., 4,726.

Boon, ready; bound. (Ice. búinn, prepared)

"Ah's *boon* ti Aubro" (Aldboro').

"And bad hem alle be *bown*, beggeres and other." P.P., II., 159.

"Hym to serue bene redy *bown*.." Psalter, 1, 14.

Botch, a sore; a little boil; also an unskilful workman, and the work he does.

"In the place of the *botch*, aperith a fel wounde." Wic., Lev., 13, 19

"Jack's a reglar *botch*; he maks a *botch* ov ivvery thing he diz."

Brass, money.

"Hez tha getten onny *brass* i' thi cleeas?" (clothes, *i.e.* pockets).

"And bere (carried) here *bras* at þi bakke." P.P., III., 195.

Brazzocks, wild mustard (charlock).

"As *brisokis* that a while in somere ere grene." Psalter, 36, 2.

Breed, (Ice., breiðr) breadth.

"What was size on't?" "Aboot *breed* o' mi hand."

A wall that is the breadth of a brick in thickness is "a brick-a-*breed* wall." (Ice., a breiðr—in breadth).

"Kyt it in smale pecys of a peny *brede*." Ck. Bk., p. 7.

"A lengthe and a *brede*." P. P., III., 202.

"The *brede* (of the ark) fifti cubits." Wic., Gen., 6, 15.

"Semely shappe of *brede* and lenthe." Pr. of Con., 5,899.

Brig, (Ice., bryggja ; A.-S., bricg ; Swed., brygga) a bridge ; as Allaman-wath Brig ; Stamford Brig, &c.

" Til that he saw him on þe *brigge*.

And bi him mani fishes ligge." Havelok, 881.

" A *brig* was ower þat gret water." Old Eng. Mis., 212, 57.

Broc, (Ice., brokkr) a badger. The word and the animal both extinct, though 30 years ago, as many as a dozen badgers, in their barrels, for baiting purposes, could be seen at Magdalen Fair, Hedon.

" Wayte nowe, he lokis like a *brokke*,

Were he in a bande (string) for to bayte." York Pl., 258, 116.

Brogues, (Ice., brók) breeches, made of leather. Obsolete, though in remote country districts the old tailors used to apply the term to trousers, and say " Ah 've getten a pair o' *brogues* ti mak bi ti-mooan at neet." The Blue-coat children, in Beverley, used to wear leather breeches, often called *brogues ;* and the last leather-breeches maker in that town was also a glover, for the gloves were leathern too. The name of Ragnar Lodbrog (Shaggy Breeches) perpetuates this word " brogue " for " breeches."

Brust, burst. Burst is formed from brust, as bird is from brid, burn from bren, or dirt from drit.

" Into termes of open outrage *brust.*" F.Q. 3, 1, 48.

" Heat that soone in flame forth *brust.*" F.Q. 3, 3, 25.

The past tense is " brast "—" He ran full butt at deear an *brast* it oppen."

" Dreadfull Furies, which their chaines have *brast.*" F.Q. 1, 5, 31.

Bunch, to kick.

" Deean't *bunch* him aboot like that."

" He *bonched* hem." P. P., Prologue, l. 74.

A farm labourer is called a *bunch*-clot (clod-kicker) by the town's people, who wish to scorn or ridicule him.

Busk, (Danish, busk ; Swed., buske ; Dutch, bosch, a wood, forest ; Old High German, busc) a bush. Nearly

obsolete, though a bush of whin (furze) is still pretty commonly called a whin *busk*.

"A *busk* I see yonder brennand bright." York Pl., 74, 101.

Caff, (A.-Sax., ceaf ; Du., kaf ; Ger., kaff) chaff, the husks
of wheat, &c.

"þe *caff* o corn he cast sumquile (while),

In þe flum (river) þat hait (called) þe nile." Curs. Mun. 4751.

"For . . . . fyre þat *caffe* son may bryn." (burn).   Pr. of
Con., 3,148.

Callit, a scold ; a virago ; a constant fault-finder.

"To make the shameless *callit* know herself."   Hy. VI.,
pt. 3, II. 2.

So we have the verb *callit; callitin*-boot—a wordy quarrel;
and the adjective *callity*.

Cap, (1) to surpass.   "He *capt* all at com at feeat ball."

(2) to puzzle.   "It *caps* me ti knaw wheear all awd meeans
gans teeah " (old moons go to).

When anything very extraordinary is spoken of it is said
"Whah, that *caps* Leatherstarn, and he *capt* the divel."

So we get *capper*, anything puzzling ; a surprising feat ;
or anything of superior quality ; also, *capping*, astonishing,
puzzling, superior.

Chavel, to chew.   Pigs, mice, &c., *chavel* straw.

"The whale then hise *chauelis* (jaws) lukeð," (locketh,
closes).   Old Eng. Mis., 16,513.

Cheer, health ; condition ; countenance.

"What *cheer*, mi hearty?" means " How are you?"

"The licnesse of his *cheer* was chaunged." Wic., Luke,
9, 29.

"His *cheere* did seem too solemne sad." F.Q., Bk. I., 1, 2.

Childher, children.

"If þou be putt fra thi reste . . . by þy *childire* be
noght angry with þame." Pr. Tr., 30, 27.

Clack, (Ice., klaka, to twitter as a swallow, to chatter as a pie, to wrangle; Mid. High Ger., klac, a crack, break, noise) gossip; persistent talk.

"Hod thi *clack*!" is a command to be silent.

"Ther quenes (women) us daze with þer *clakke*." York Pl. 344, 211.

Clart, stickiness; feigned affection; to trifle or bungle.

(1) "This threeacle-pot is *clarty*."

(2) A father will say jokingly to his child "It's neeah use thoo kissin ma; thoo dizn't luv ma! It's all *clart*."

(3) "Ah can't bide (bear) ti see em *clartin* aboot; Ah'd rayther deeah wahk mi-sen."

(4) "Ther was ower mich *clartment* (fuss) fo' me. Ah likes things quiet."

Perhaps the most expressive word of this batch is that applied to one who makes hypocritical professions of affection, and who is termed a *clart-pooak*.

Clap, (Ice. klappa, to pat), to strike.

"And siþe *clapte* him on þe crune, (crown)
So that he stan-ded fel þor dune. (stone dead fell there down)." Havelok, 1818.

"þe sixte wende for to fle,
And he *clapte* him with þe tre(wood,stick)."Havelok,1820.

Clew, a ball of twine, worsted, &c. Old Eng. Mis. 95, 72, has *clew* for bow-string.

Click, to snatch, clutch.

"He *click'd* it oot o' mi hand."

"An (if) I *cleke* yowe, I schall felle yow."York Pl., 280,240.

Cloot, (Ice., klutr), a patch; a cloth. Female attire is sometimes styled cloots, as "Get thi *cloots* on!" A Holderness swain, who was overheard enquiring into the accomplishments of his sweetheart, asked, among other things, "Can tha set a *cloot* on a shet (shirt) wivoot puckerin (wrinkling)."

"His garment nought but many ragged *clouts*." F.Q., I, 9, 36.

"They wesshen hym and wyped hym, and wonden hym in *cloutes*." P.P., II., 220.

Cobble, (Ice. koppusteinn, a round stone), a round stone; a small boulder : to throw stones.

These water-worn boulders used to be extensively used as paving stones ; and, if for foot passengers only, seemed as if they would last till domesday ; for, being uneven, they were avoided as much as possible.   Many churches in Holderness are built of these *cobbles*, with stone dressings ; and houses, too, have them in their walls.   A "roondy" piece of coal is called a *cob*.

"Two *cobill* notis (nuts) uppon a bande." York Pl., 122, 112.

Cock, a little heap.

"Under the hay*cock* fast asleep." Nursery Rhyme.

"Under the *cocked* hay." Sh. Cal. (November)

Cock-loft, a garret in the roof.

"His *cock-loft* is unfurnished." Eng. Prov., 213.

Collops, slices of bacon.

"I have no salt bacon,
    coloppes for to maken." P.P., VI., 286.

Collop keeaks, or bacon keeaks, are made similar to a sandwich, with two layers of pastry, having bacon or ham between.

Collop Munda, the Monday before Shrove Tuesday, is so called because of its being the last day of flesh-eating before Lent, when fresh meat was cut into *collops*, and salted, to hang till Lent was over.

Cool, (Ice. kúla) a swelling on the head, caused by a blow.

"He raised a *cool* as big as a pidgin egg."

Cratch, a standing rack for hay ; a frame on which sheep are killed.

"And laide hym (Jesus) in a *cratch*." Wic., Luke, 2, 7.

Crawlin things, insect vermin.

"Wiþ crepinge *croulis* in his bak." Curs. Mun., 3,567.

Croose, lively, elated.

"Summe grop tre, and sum grop ston,
And drive hem ut, þei weren *crus,*
So (as) dogges ut of milne-hous." Havelok, 1,965.

Crud, curd. Hence *cruddle,* to curdle.

"With *cruddy* bloud congealed." F.Q., I, 5, 29.

"two grene cheses, a fewe *cruddes* and creem,
and an haver cake,
And two loues of benes and bran." P.P., VI, 283.

"Take a faire lynen clothe, and presse the *cruddes* thereon." Ck. Bk., 86.

Daft, stupid; witless.

"I compt (account) thame *daft,* an mekill worse nor mad." Lauder, 12,267.

Dag, to sprinkle. (Ice. dögg, dew).

"*Dag* cawsey (path) afooar tha sweeps it." A housewife also *dags* the dried clothes previous to folding and ironing them.

Dale, a valley. Valley, as a place name, is unknown; but dales abound; as, Danesdale, Kendale, Slaysdale, Welton Dale, York Dale, Whitedale, Thixendale, Grindall, and the *Dale* towns.

"So þat þe erthe bothe downe and *dale.*" York Pl., 10, 30.

Deng or **Ding,** (Ice. dengja, to beat), to throw with violence.

"But *dyng* þam doune, Tylle all be dede." York Pl., 91, 399.

"For he *dynges* out the deuyl." Psalter, 504, 2.

Dess, a heap or pile of potatoes, fruit, &c.

"There was a rare *dess* o' taties i' cooaner, bud sumhoo or uther it didn't last lang eneeaf."

Dhrop, (Ice. drepe, a blow), to knock down

"Behave thi-sen, or Ah'll *dhrop* tha."

"Summe of you shall ich (I) *drepen.*" Havelok, 1783.

Didher, to tremble; to shake with cold.

"My flesshe *dyderis.*"   York Pl., 240, 2.

Dill, to assuage pain ; to deaden.

Medicine given to infants, to deaden pain, is called *dill* water.

"How Iuus (Jews) wit þer gret vnschill,
Wend (strove) his uprising to *dill.*" Curs. Mun., 202.

Din, (Ice. dynr), noise.

" þan began gret *dine* to rise,
For þe laddes on ilke wise,
Him assayleden wit grete *dintes.*" Havelok, 1860.

"And leve thy *dyne.*" York Pl., 42, 80.   Not greatly different to "Hod thi *din* ! "

Dodher, to shake with cold, or fear.

"It's plaguey cawd ; Ah's all ov a *dodher.*"

"Thoo *dodherin* awd thing !" A contemptuous expression.

Dollup, a heap ; a lump.

"Ay ! what a dollup o' dumplin !"

Dowills, felloes ; sections of the rim of a wheel.

"The spokis and *dowlis* of the wheelis." Wic., III Kings, 7, 33.

Een, eyes.

"Shed thy faire beames into my feeble *eyne.*"   F. Q., Bk. I., Prol. IV.

Egg, to sharpen ; to incite.   .

"Adam and Eue he *egged* on to ille."   P. P., I., 65.

"Til whilk (to which) þai *egged* þam, bathe night and day."
Pr. of Con., 5,483.

" I am sorie of a sight
þat *egges* me to ire." York Pl., 256, 40.

Efther, (Ice., eftir) after.

"Ilke (each) warke *eftyr* is wroghte."   York Pl., 6, 125.

"*Eftyr* thar inclinaciouns."   R. R., 77, 6.

"*Eftyr* a faa (few) dayes he apperyde till (to) ane þat was famyliare till (to) hym in hys life." Pr. Tr., 7, 4.

Feeath—hesitating; reluctant.

"When Ah gat ti knaw spot was hanted, Ah was varry *feeath* o' gannin."

Fettle, or *Fittle*, to prepare; arrange; make fit. So "*fit*" means ready; also, an arrangement of stanzas, or parts of a poem.

"Is taties *fit*?"

"Ah 'll gan an *fittle* dinner noo."

"*Fettled* him to shoot." Per. Rel., 65.

Fey, (Ice., fægja, to cleanse), to winnow; to cleanse corn from the chaff and dust.

"Give uz ken-crewk (churn-handle) for *feyin*-machine, we 're gannin ti *fey* cooan."

"Oates threshed and *feyed*." Best, 4.

Flay, (Ice., flaga), to frighten; to make afraid.

"With þe left hand þam to *flay*." Pr. of Con., 1268.

"Hym for to tempte and for to *flay*." Pr. of Con., 2247.

A scare-crow is termed a *flay*-krake.

Flit, (Ice., flyta; Dan. flytte), to pass away; to remove.

"A sandie hill, that still did *flitt* and fall away." F. Q., I., 4, 5.

"My ffadir is bowne to *flitte*." York Pl., 47, 68.

The bat, from its changeful motion, is called a *flitter*-mouse.

Fog, after-math; the growth of grass after the hay harvest.

"We 've had lots o' meeat this back end (autumn), *fog* was ommast as lang as midda." (meadow).

"The *fogge* of this close (field) letten for 33s. 4d." Best, 130.

Fond, silly; foolish.

"Now Noye (Noah) in faythe, þe *fonnes* (goes *fond*) full faste." York Pl., 48, 89.

"Fooles þat are *fonde*." York Pl., 303, 329.

"He 's a *fond* chapman that comes the day after the fair." Eng., Prov., p. 207.

"Ordinances of her owen *fonnyd* heeads." (*fond* heads). Wic. Works, 3, 9.

Fooar-eldhers, fore-fathers.

"Yr *for-eldres* þe bible wrat." Curs., Mun., 14,399.

Fra, (Ice., fra), from.

"And *fro* that our the disciple took her in." Wic., Jno., 19, 27.

"Puttes vayne ocupacyons *fra* us." Pr. Tr., 3., 14.

Freshwood, threshold ; a piece of wood across the bottom of the doorway, to keep out the *freshes*, or overflowings of water after rain.

"Noo, mahnd an deeant threead uppa *freshwood*."

Frush, to rush.

"Alto shiuere and alto *frusshe*." Havelok, 1993.

Full smack, (1) headlong; heavily.

"Ah fell *full smack* o' mi feeace "

(2) with determination.

"He gans at it *full smack*."

Fullock, (1) violent energy.

"Oss went at yat (gate) wiv a reg'lar *fullock*, an brast it reet offa crewks."

(2) To jerk violently. Boys at marbles, to prevent their opponents using undue force, cry out "Neeah *fullocks* !"

Fulth, sufficiency. Formed like warm-th, leng-th, &c.

"We 'd plenty ti it (eat) an we all it (ate) ti wer *fulth*."

"Its *fulth* of milk." Best, 5.

Gain, (Ice. gegn, convenient), near, convenient.

"The *ganest* gate (nearest way) þat i gane go." York Pl. 59, 90.

A *gain* way of doing anything is an expeditious way of doing it.

Gan or **Gang,** (Ice. ganga), to go.

"Noo, *gan* on, an hod thi noise."

"On grounde ongaynely may y *gange*." York Pl., 32, 99.

"There 's been sum fahn (some fine) *gannins* on amang em."

"They live at a odd hoose, bud they 've plenty ov cummers an *ganners*." (Occasional visitors ; persons who call when passing).

Garth, (Ice. garð), a yard ; an enclosure ; an orchard ; as fawd-*garth* (fold-yard), stag*gath* (stack-yard), &c.

"In keepinge of appil (apple) *garths*." Psalter, 78, 1.

A road at Bridlington, which led to the orchard of the Priory Church, before the dissolution of the monasteries, is still called Apple-*garth* Lane.

Gate, (1) (Ice. gata), a way ; a road. In Driffield, Nafferton, Cranswick, &c., streets are called *gates*, even where there have never been any *gates*, (doors, bars, &c.) in connection with them. The gate, which barred the way, took its name from the way it barred. See Stee and Stile.

"Agaynes kyndly oys (use) or oþer *gates*." Pr. Tr., 11.

(2) A right of pasturage, &c. Local advertisements notify *gaits* for cattle, &c.

(3) Manner ; method.

"Weel, gan yer awn *gate*!" (Do as you please).

Gaum, (Ice. guma, to take heed), sense ; wit ; tact. Is it not closely akin to gauma, a man ?

"He hezn't a bit o' *gaum* aboot him."

"He was that *gaumless* he let him hev it for a pund less then he ga fo 't."

"Have ӡe geten vs þis *gome*," (man). York Pl., 154, 255.

"Sco (she) was giuen to zebedei,
A daughti *gom* (man) o' galilee." Curs. Mun., 12697.

Gavlac, (a diminutive from Ice. gaffall, a dung-fork) a crowbar ; a lever.

"One recon, one *gavelocke*, one fier shole." Best, 172.

Gen, to repine ; to weep. Akin to "grin."

"He's *genniest* chap uppo yath ; he's awlas *gennin*."

"His face was ugly, and his countenance sterne,
That could have frayed one with the very sight,
And gaped like a gulf when he did *gerne* "
F.Q. 5, 12, 15.

Getten, p. p. of "to get "

"He's *getten* all he wanted."

"And has *getyn* a som dele ryste "   Pr. Tr. 17.

Gif, if.

"*Gif* they axe wheear Ah cum fra."

"*Gyf* Christ had nocht as-cendit." Lauder, 12, 283.

Gift i' gob, fluency of speech.

"Oor pahson hez a rare *gift i' gob.*"

Glooar, (Ice. glora, to stare), to stare rudely.

"Go hense, þou *glorand* (glooaring) geldyng."   York Pl., 126, 157.

Glowpin, (Ice., glopr, to stare; gloppen, to stupefy), staring with amazement.   Almost obsolete.

"þis tre sho (she) stert al *gloppened* fra." Curs. Mun., 8901.

Golly or **Gollock,** an unfledged bird.

"A nest of briddis . . . . and the moder of the *gollis.*" Wic., Deut., 22, 6.

When the young birds have left the nest, they are said to be "fligged an flown."

Grave, "He went ti *grave* gahdin (garden) ower, an when he'd *groven* it, pigs gat in an paddled it doon ageean."

"He up *grofe* it, and he fell in the pit that he made." Psal. 7, 16

Greeas, (1) grease. Figuratively, flattery.

"What a awd *greeas* horn that fella is ! He thried ti *greease* ma up, an get ma ti buy summat."

(2) gain, profit, advantage.

"He weeant gether mitch *greeas* oot o' that."

Grub, to toil ; to delve ; to dig up roots, &c.

"And made hym *grubble* and grave." York Pl., 46, 23

Grund, ground, earth ; to grind ; pt.t., did grind.

"The stone on which knives &c. are ground is termed a *grun*-stan."

"Scarp (sharp) *grunden* knijf in hand he bar (bore)." Curs. Mun., 21, 437.

Grip, a gutter ; a narrow ditch.   That which has *hold* upon the land ; so *gripe*, a pain in the bowels,

FOLK SPEECH OF EAST YORKSHIRE.

"men casten hem in poles, (pools)
Or in a *grip*, or in þe fen." Havelok, 2101.
" And summe leye in dikes, (ditches)
And summe in *gripes*." Havelok, 1923.

Grape, p. t. of Grasp, to clutch ; also p. t. of Grope, touch,
feel.

" Hend (hands) thai hafe, and thai sall noghte *grape*."
Psalter, 113, 15.

" Ah *grape* mi way i' dahk an ommast tummell'd ower
yat stowp." (gate post).

Hack, (Du., hakken ; Dan., hakke ; Swed., hacka ; Ger.,
hacken, to chop), to cut or chop in small pieces.   A
stammerer is called a *hackerer*, for he cuts his words in pieces.

" He *hackers* and stammers seeah, that yan can't tell what
he meeans."

Mince-meat is known as *hack*-meat ; the knife with which
it is made is a *hacking*-knife ; and the trough or block on
which the work is performed is a *hacking*-trough, or *hacking*-
block.

" Putte þerto Percely (parsley), Sawge leufs, nogt to smal
hakkyd." (Sage leaves not too small hacked). Ck. Bk., 32, 22.

Haft or Heft, handle, or the part by which you *have* a
thing.

"The yren slipt of fro the *haft*." Wic., Deut., 19, 5.

" For other *haftis* in hand have we." York Pl., 158, 76.

[The Glossary of the Plays gives " affairs " as the meaning
of " haftis."]

Hales, handles of ploughs, wheel-barrows, &c. ; *i.e.* the
part by which you *hale* (haul). See Acts, 8, 3, (A.V.) " Saul
. . . . *haling* men and women, committed them to prison."

" Not to trouble themselves with *haling* on so much at
once. ' Best, 50.

Hansel, (Ice. handsal, earnest-money), first money, or first
use.

" Ah sall *hansel* mi new bonnet o' Sunda."

E

"The catchpole is the first *handsel* of the young rapiers of the templars."   Micro., 142.

Hanted, haunted.   Hence "hant" means a habit.

"He's getten a *hant* o' gannin there ivvery neet."

> "Mont olivet it es an hill
> þat iesus (Jesus) *hanted* mickel till (to)."
>
> Curs. Mun., 13,690.

Happin, covering ; bed-clothes.

"Ah was cawd las neet ; Ah hadn't hauf aneeaf *happin*."

"Hille (pile) on me *happing*."   York Pl., 257, 82.

"And I sall *happe* þe, myn owne dere childe."

York Pl., 116. 120.

"Thou reft him all the *happinge* that he had."

Psalter, 5. 10. 20.

Hard, (1) quickly.

"And *harde* to her I wil me hye."   York Pl., 22, 15.

(2) fast ; tight.

"Bunden *hard* wit rapes strang."   Curs. Mun., 21003.

Harden, to incite.

"When lads was fightin, Tom *harden'd* em on all he could."

> " Her nourslings did with mutinous uprore
> *Harten* against her selfe her conquer'd spoile,
> Which she had wonne from all the world afore "
>
> Spenser.   [Ruins of Rome, 22].

Hask, (1) (Ice. hask, rigorous), stiff ; unyielding.

"*Harsk* and harde."   Curs. Mun., 21,343.

(2) bitter, tart, *harsh* to the taste.

"Give uz anuther lump o' seeagur (sugar) teeah's si *hask*."

Heeeam, home.

" For she would cal him often *heame* " Sh. Cal. (November)

Heeap, a great number of persons or things.

"There was a *heeap* o' fooaks at chotch."

"There's a *heeap* ov apples uppa that three."

" Ah've been ti Hull *heeaps* o' tahms."

"Bot fare-wele all þe *heppe* (crowd)." York Pl., 150. 132.

Hick, to hitch ; an upward jerk.

"*Hick* it up a bit higher."

Farmers, maltsters, and others, use an oblong frame, called a *hickin*-barra, by which a sack of corn can be lifted from the ground by two men, who seize hold of the "hales " and "*hick* " it up, on to the back of him who carries it to the wagon, &c.

Hing, to hang. A poor lean miserable thing is termed a "*hing*-lug."

> "And bot þai me þaire broþer bringe,
> For soþ þair ostage salle I *hing*." Curs. Mun., 4991.
> (Joseph sending for Benjamin).

"Thys frute full styll sall *hyng*." York Pl., 20. 78.

I is, I am. The verb present indicative singular being Ah is, Thoo is, He is.

"Ah 's (I is) varry cawd ! Give uz sum wahm teeah."

"þe man ye seke, he said, *es i*." Curs., Mun., 19,904.

Jowl, to knock together.

"Ah 'll *jowl* thi heead an wall tegither."

"þat none jangill nor *jolle* at my gate." York Pl. 307. 14.

Kep, to catch anything thrown or falling.

Shrove Tuesday is called *Keppin* Day, because part of the amusement consists of *kepping* balls.

> "Horn in is (his) armes hire *kepte*, (caught)."
> King Horn, 1208.

"And *kipte* (caught) up þat heui ston." Havelok, 1050.

Kessen, p.p. of to *cast; cast off*.

"Hez tha onny *kessen* cleeas ti give away ?"

> "Soth, quat has þou in þi hand ?
> Laured, he said, i ber a wand.
> þou *kest* it on þe gress, i bidd,
> Gladli, laured, and sua he didd."
> Curs. Mun., 5809.—(Moses at the burning bush).

" Truly, what hast thou in thine hand ?
Lord, he said, I bear a wand.
Thou cast it on the grass, I bid ;
Gladly, Lord, and so he did."

Kinnle, to produce young ; literally, to bring forth the same *kind.* Said only of rabbits ; but Wicliffe has, in Luke, 3, 7, "*Kyndlyngis* of eddires ;" and Shakespeare, in " As you like it," III. 2., has "The cony that you see dwell where she was *kindled."* When we *kindle* a fire do we not produce fire ?

Kist, a chest ; a large box.

"And laid in *kist* o' marbil stan." Curs. Mun. 21,018.

Kitlin, (Ice. ketlingr), a kitten. Formed from cat, as birdling, nestling, gosling, from bird, nest, and goose respectively.

"It ought not to be said that Cats, but that *Kitlings* have nine lives." Lister.

Kittle, (Ice. kitla), to tickle.

At a church, in East Holderness, the clerk, finding himself singing the Psalms alone, suddenly stopt, and exclaimed, "If ya deean't help ma, Ah can't gan on ; Ah 've getten a *kitlin* i' mi throoat."

"*Kitlynge* of thair flesch." Psalter, 2. 4.

Kittle, (1) delicate, sensitive.

"It 's as *kittle* as a moose-thrap."

"If an ewe bee *kittle* on her yower (udder) let her dance in a payre of hopples." Best, 80.

(2) critical ; difficult to decide.

"Ah deean't knaw what ti say ; it 's a *kittlish* coshan." (question).

Krake, a crow. A scare-crow is called a flay-*crake* ; and the land-rail is a corn-*crake.*

" When it is all waxen blake, the *krake* nuryssis (nourishes) it as his aghyn (own) bird." Psalter, 146. 10.

Lake, (Ice. leikr, a game; leika, to play).

"Noo, lads; let's (let us) *lake* at tig."

"And gif him list for to *laike.*" P.P., Prol. 172.

"How þis losell (rascal) *laykis* with his lord."

York P., 250. 253.

"Begunnen þer for to *layke.*" Havelok, 1011.

Lall, to protrude.

"He *lalled* oot his tung, an meead feeaces at ma."

"And *lilled* forth his bloody flaming tong." F.Q., I., 5. 34.

Lane, to teach.

"Is this God's wourd that *larnis* thame this euyle."

Lauder, 16. 618.

"How þou *lernist* þe peple." P.P., IV. 11.

Lap, to wrap.

"*Lap* it up, an put it away."

"That daintie Rose . . . . *lapped* up her silken leaves." F.Q., I., 5. 34.

"þat he before was *lapped* in." Pr. of Con., 523.

Late, (Ice. leita), to seek; to search for.

"Ah *lated* it hauf an hoor, an cudn't find it."

"Nowe (may) god neuer *late* man after me."

York Pl., 34. 149.

Lathe or **Leeath,** (Ice. hlað), a barn.

"Let's gan inti *leeath* ti lake."

Lee, lie; falsehood.

"Mare thoo sez, an mare *lees* thoo tells."

"That þow be never leif (at liberty) to *lee.*" R. R., 92. 51.

Leeath-wake, (Ice., liðr, limb) supple-limbed; used also in reference to corpses which do not become rigid in the usual time.

Leeav, soon; rather.

"Ah'd as *leeav* deeah this as that."

"A! I am full werie, lefe (soon) late (let) me slepe."

Yk. Pl., 110. 249.

Leet, to alight. The past tense is "let."

"A clude (cloud) þat þar again (against) him *light.*"
Curs. Mun., 18,767.

"A cat awlas *leets* ov it feet."

Lig, (Ice. liggja), to lie, as in bed ; to place down.

"He say (saw) his wyues modir *liggynge.*"
Wic., Matt., 8. 14.

"But firste I wille *lygge* on (place on) my lyne."
York Pl., 43. 98.

"Learne to *ligge* soft." Sh. Cal., (May).

"þer bermen let he alle *ligge.*" Havelok, 876.

A sluggard is known as a *lig*-i'-bed ; and when the moon rises later at night it is said "Meean *ligs* in a bit noo o' neets."

To expend money is to *lig* it out ; and the same term is used in preparing a corpse for burial.

Lin, (Ice. lín), linen. *Lin* is the flax plant ; *lin*seed its seed ; and *lin*en the product of its manufacture.

"He dranc neuer cisar (cider) ne wine,
Ne wered (wore) neuer clath o' *line.*" Curs. Mun., 12679.

The York Plays, p. XXVII., gives *lynweuers* as the name of a guild of artisans.

Litha, verb imp., (Ice. hlyða, to listen), harken ! listen !

"*Litha,* lutha, luxtha ; let s gan an lake on hossin-clog, (play on the log from which horses are mounted)."

Sitha ! and sutha ! (see thou) are similar expressions.

"And seyde liþes (listen) nou alle to me."
Havelok, 1400.

"*Litheth* and lesteneth." (Harken ye and listen ye). Gam., 1.

Liver, deliver.

"Carrier had a beeap o' things, bud he gat em all *livered.*"

"She gladly did of that same babe accept,
As of her owne by *liverey.*" F. Q., 6. 4. 37.

" Gamelyn," seyde Adam, "for seynte charite,
Pay large *lyuerey* for the loue of me." Gam., 513.

Livered, delivered.

"Carrier *livered* em all, wivoot a mistak."

"And *liverd* þaim fra pharaon." Curs. Mun. 14403.

Lop, a flea.

Named from its *louping* (leaping) powers.

"Grete *loppis* ouere alle þis lande þei flee."
York P., 85. 293.

Lopper, (Ice. laupa, to congeal), to curdle.

"*Lopird* is as mylke thaire hert . . . . but in
lopirynge it waxis soure." Psalter, 118. 70.

" He had na other fode (food),
Bot wlatsom glet (loathsome slime) and *lopyrd* blode."
Pr. of Con., 459.

Loup, (Ice., hlaupa), to leap, to jump.

Boys play at *loup*-back, *i.e.* leap-frog.

"And bigan til (to) him to *loupe*." Havelok, 1801.

" With that sprong forth a naked swayne,
With spotted winges, like Peacocks trayne
And laughing *lope* to a tree." Sh. Cal., (March).

" . . . . . building churches and *louping* over them."
Hazlitt's Proverbs, p. 224.

"*Lopp*estere (lobster) and drie haddok." Ck., Bk., 114, 28.
for the lobster is the leaper, or louper.

Louse, loose.

One free from his apprenticeship is said to be *lowse*, and
the supper given on that occasion is a "*lowzenin feeast.*" A
lowse hand is a workman who can be conveniently spared.
A *lowseness* is the diarrhœa. To "*lowze* oot" is to
unharness.

"*Lous* him (Lazarus) nu, he said." Curs. Mun., 14,356.

"To *louse* the thwong of his schoo." Wic., Jno. I. 27.

Low, (Ice., log, a flame; and loga, to flame), a flame; to
blaze.

The dancing flames of a fire are called lilli-*lows*.

"Of *lowe* and reke with stormes melled." (mixed).

Pr. of Con., 9431.

"In that *low* sa dim."   Curs. Mun., 23,232.

"a . . . . sight to se
him (Moses) þougte brennynge a tre,
As hit wiþ *loue* al were bileyde " (be-laid).

Curs. Mun., 5,739.

Mak, (Ice., maki), a mate ; a companion.

*Mak*less has become matchless—a shortened form of *make* ; as tak for take, and mak for make (verb).

A father, rebuking his son for taking a worthless fellow as his companion, will say, "Deean't gan wiv him.   He's nooa sooat ov a *mak* fo thoo."

"But he has made to (for) hym a *make*."   York Pl., 22. 14.

"As true as turtle to her *make*."   F. Q., 3. 11. 2.

    "But (except) thou hire take
    þat y wole geuen þe to *make*."   Havelok, 1,149.

"She is fayne of þi felawship for to be þi *make*."

P. P., III. 18.

In All Saints' Church, Hereford, there was a tablet with an inscription (1428).

    "Here lyeth under this stone, William Wake,
    And by him Joane, his wife and *make*."

Bardsley's Surnames, p. 475.

Mang, (Ice. menga, to mingle), to break, bruise, crush, mix.

A child who, instead of eating his food, might be picking it and pushing it about his plate, would be reprimanded by his mother thus "Deean't *mang* it aboot seeah."

"Take sugre and poudre Gynger, and *meng* it with þe farcere, (stuffing.")   Ck. Bk., 46. 10.

Mare, more.

"þat we suld hald it (sabbath) euer *mare*." Curs. Mun., 410.

"All wondered on him, less and *mare*." Curs. Mun., 13,886.
"He sall euer *mare* be withowttyn joye." Pr. Tr., p. 4.
Maste, most.
"*Maste* spedfull *maste* medfull and faire." Pr. Tr., p. 26.
Mene, or **Meny,** a family.

Quite obsolete in common speech, but is still preserved in
an old rhyme, used in stationing boys at the various "hods,"
preparatory to a game.

> "*Meny, meny*, miny mo,
> I ax ya wheear mun this man go?
> Sum gans eeast, an sum gans west,
> An sum gans ower the high crake nest."

"How he sholde his *meine* fede."   Havelok, 827.

Mense, (Ice. menska, decency), (1) the best part; the
original freshness and beauty.

"Ay! lass! all *mense* is offa thah best bonnit."

(2) decency; manners.

"That lass hez neeather sense nor *mense*."

(3) to grace; to adorn; to honour.

"Mah wod, Jack, bud thoo did lewk weel o' Sethada neet,
wiv a lass ov eeather sahd ti *mense* tha off."

"Gif I may, as I mygte, *menske* þe with giftes."

                                      P.P., III., 183.

Menseless means without decency or manners.
Middin, a heap; a dunghill.
"Als (as) well on *myddyng* als on more."

                                      York Pl., 85. 296.

"A fouler *myddyng* saw þow never nane."

                                      Pr. of Con., 628.

Milt, (Ice. milti), the spleen of an animal; sometimes
called a cat collap.

"Take pipes, hertes, *myltes*, and rybbes of þe swyne."

                                      Ck. Bk. 70. 30.

"Nv schal for-roteyn	Now shall to rot
þine teþ and þi tunge	Thy teeth and thy tongue,
þi Mawe and þi *Milte*	Thy stomach, and thy milt,
þi lyure and þi lunge	Thy liver, and thy lung,
And þi þrote bolle,	And the swelling of thy throat
þat þu mide sunge,	That thou singest with."

Old. Eng. Mis., 179. 169.

Mind, a resolve ; a determination.

"Ah 've a good *mind* nut ti gan at all."

"To him that *mindes* (resolves) his chance t' abye."

F. Q., Bk. II. 4. 40.

Mizzle, fine drizzling rain.

"Now gynnes to *mizzle*, hye we homeward fast."

Sh. Cal. (Nov).

"If the morninge bee wette and *mislinge*." Best, 44.

Moel, mole ; a dark-coloured spot.

"Diz tha knaw Tom hez a *mooel* on his ayme."

"Upon the little brest, like christall bright,
  She mote perceive a little purple *mold*." F. Q., 6. 12. 7.

Mought, might, p. t. of May.

"Iche man *mut* nedis shryuen oonys (once) in þe yer."

Wic. Works, p. 329.

Mouther, or **Moother**, toll in kind, taken by millers.

The custom is quite obsolete and the word seldom heard. A miller who was suspected of helping himself too liberally was said to "knaw hoo ti moother."

"The miller taketh more *mowter* than is his due." Best, 103.

Mowdiewarp, or **Mowthad**, (Ice., moldvarpa), a mole.

"And a *mold werp*." Wic., Lev., XI., 30.

"Like *Moldwarps* nousling." Spenser, p. 556.

Muck, (1) dirt.

"But *mucky* filth his braunching armes annoyes."

F. Q., Bk. II., 7. 15.

(2) manure. A *muck heeap* is a manure heap, and so is a *muck middin.* To *muck oot* is to clear out manure.

(3) figuratively, dirt.   Wicliffe is very partial to this
word.   In his Testament and other works it is in regular
use for wealth, &c.

"To geten worldely *muk* more þan soule helþe." (health).
Wic. Works, p. 5.

" þei prechen principally for worldeli *muk.*"
Wic. Works, p. 10.

Mull, to spoil by bad workmanship.

Mullock, a piece of work spoilt by bad workmanship.

"He framed sa badly at job, Ah thowt he wad mak a
mullock on 't."

Mun, (Ice., munu), must.

" Ah *mun* be off heeam."

" He *mon* be brought down with sorrow." Psalter, 9. 42.

"Thai *mun* fynd it."   Psalter, 24. 12.

Neeaf, (Ice., hnefi), the fist.   Hence *nevill,* to strike with
the fist.

" With þe *neue* he robert sette
    Biforn þe teth a dint ful strong." Havelok, 2,404.

" Of that bignesse that one may thrust in theire *neafe.*"
Best, 126.

Noddle, the head.

"Thoo 's soft i' thi *noddle.*"

" þose *noddil* on hym with neffes,
    þat he (do) noghte nappe." York Pl., 268. 370.

(Strike him on the head with fists, so that he sleeps not).

Nope, (1) the head.   Akin to knop, knob.

(2) to strike on the head. See p. 28.

The children have a saying, " Bells is ringing, cats is singing, an dogs is gannin ti chotch," which represents a departed
custom.   When the church bells were ringing for service,
the cats were left at home, to bask before the fire, and sing
"three-thrums" on the hearth-rug; while the dogs went to
church with their masters, and lay under the seat of the pew
until the service was over.   Though usually quiet, they were

not always so, and an official was appointed to keep the tiresome ones in order. He was termed a dog-*noper*, and was armed with a stick, bearing a like name.

It is related that on one occasion, a fight began near the pulpit, between two dogs of unequal size ; and, in spite of the dog-*noper*, increased in intensity, until, by reason of noise and excitement, the preacher was compelled to cease preaching. Women stood on the seats for safety, the men in order to see better, and all thoughts of place and time were lost in the common excitement. Finally, the parson leaned over the edge of the pulpit, clapping his hands and saying "Two ti one on lahtle un ! Two ti one on lahtle un !"

Other some, others.

"Sum fooaks is wahse ti pleease then *other sum*."

"Maria his moder and oþer sum." Curs. Mun., 18875.

Otther, to talk foolishly ; to wander aimlessly.

A prolific and forceful word. A slow-witted person is *ottherin* ; an *otther-pooak* is literally a poke (sack) of *otther* (nonsense) ; and an *otther-kite* (stomach) or *otther-skeeat* is somewhat the same ; and so is *otthertyhoy*.

Owmly, (Ice. aumligr), (1) lonely, dismal, dreary, as applied to localities.

(2) lonely and spacious, as applied to houses, &c. Almost like " dowly," (*i.e.* dole-ly).

" Ah sudn't like ti sleep wi mi-sen i' that greeat *owmly* hoose."

Pale or **Pail**, a rail.

"Noo, keep offa them *palins*."

"She is ybrought unto a *paled* greene." F.Q., Bk. 1, c. 5.

"And stood at his garden *pale*." Per. Rel., p. 75.

Pan, to become adapted by use. A new boot is not comfortable until it *pans* to the foot.

As a man becomes accustomed to his work he *pans* to it.

Two people, living together, have to *pan* one to the other, before smoothness is possible.

That which will become well adapted, or will fit properly by use, is *panable.*

Pawk, (Ice., puki; a goblin), insolent impertinent talk.

"Noo lets he' neean o' thi *pawk,* thoo *pawky* young raggill."

Pet, offence.

"He taks *pet* at ivvery thing yan sez or diz."

"He now takes *pet.*" Earle's Mic., p. 20.

One who has had all his *pets* or fits of ill temper indulged to excess is said to be "*pettled.*"

Pissimire, pis-mire, the red ant. So called because it discharges a reddish fluid.

Pooak, sack; bag; pouch. Pocket is a diminutive of *poke.*

"Nivver thoo buy a pig iv a *pooak.*"

"His neather lip was not like man nor beast,

But like a wide deepe *poke,* down hanging low."F. Q., 4.7.6.

Possessed, held; controlled. Though not a dialect word, its peculiar use in the dialect justifies its appearance here.

"Ah deean't knaw what *possessed* ma, when Ah did it."

Pucker, to gather in folds or wrinkles. Literally, to make into pokes or small bags.

"She's *puckered* up this sowin shamfully. It'll all he' ti cum oot ageean."

Puddle, a muddy place. Connected with *pool.*

"Ah'll skelp tha weel, thoo mucky thing! Thoo's been thruf ivvery *puddle* thoo cud find."

"And like to troubled *puddles* have them made."

Spenser (Teares of the Muses) 276.

Purchass, leverage; advantage.

"Ah can't stor it wi this gavlac, for Ah can get neeah *purchass.*"

Quietsome, (1) still; not restless. A *quietsome* bayn, (child.)

(2) tranquil. A *quietsome* neet.

(3) not quarrelsome. He's a *quietsome* chap.

Raggill, a rascal,

"And farre away, amid their *rakehell* bands,
They spiede a lady, left all succour lesse." F. Q., 5. 11. 44.

Rake, (Ice. reika), to ramble about idly.

"He gans *rakin* aboot cunthry asteead o' gettin on wiv his wahk."

"Thai suffire thaire hert to *rake* in ydel thoghtes."
Psalter, 85. 5.

Rame, (Ice. remja), to cry out; to shout.

"He *ramed* oot at ma."

"mit (with) te *rem* ðat he maked." Old Eng. Mis., 1. 22.

Ramp, to stamp about; to scold furiously.

". . . . . . their bridles they would champ,
And trampling . . . . would fiercely *ramp*."
F.Q., Bk. I., c. 5.

Reek, (Ice. reykr), smoke.   Akin to "roke"—sea mist.

"It was all ov a *reek*, like a lahm-kill" (lime-kiln.)

"For the *reek* it smithers me." Per. Rel., 79.

"Few chymneis *reeking* you shall espye." Sh. Cal.

Remmon, or **Remmle,** to remove.

"O, y'u needn't *remmon*; Ah can manidge."

"Wot no man þe time wanne he sal hennce *rimen*."

(No man knows the time when he removes hence, *i.e.* dies).   Proverbs of Alfred.—Old Eng. Mis., 113. 170.

Render, (Ice. renna), to make run, to melt.

"The (golden) kalfe thai *rendid*." Psalter, 15. 19.

The leaves of fat from the inside of a pig are *rendered*, to make lard.   That which is left after the liquid fat is poured off, is termed "scraps"; out of which "scrap-keeaks" are made.

Rensh, rinse; wash out.

"And *rynsche* þin dysshe alle abowte with oyle."
Ck. Bk., 24. 6.

Rig, (Ice. hryggr), (1) ridge of a house, stack, &c.   The piece of wood forming the ridge is called the *rig* three (*i.e.* ridge-tree).

(2) the highest part of a section of ploughing.

(3) the back, or backbone.

"þat his *rigg* on it may reste." York Pl., 339. 73.

"Bernard stirt (started) up, þat was full big,
And cast a brinie (cuirass) upon his *rig*."
Havelok, 1774.

Rock, a distaff. Quite obsolete, because the spinning wheel has disappeared, but very old people still remember it, though to mention it to them, forcibly reminds them how very old they are.

"Sad cloths held the *rocke*, the whiles the thrid (thread) was spun with paine." F. Q., 4. 2. 48.

Roosin, (1) (Ice., hrósa), boasting.

"What *rosyng* (boasting) of riches."

"I cried . . . . *rosand* (to boast) me of rightwisness."
Psalter, 31. 3.

(2) of large size.

"That's a *roozin* lee." (lie).

Ryme, (Ice. hrím), hoar. A *rime* frost is a hoar frost, or a white frost.

"And he sloghe in haghil (hail) the vyners (vines) and thaire mours (mulberries) in *ryme* froist." Psalter, 77. 52.

Sad, heavy, as unleavened.

"*Sad* keeaks" and dip form a favourite breakfast.

"Bete on þe cloth with a ladell to make *sad*."
Ck. Bk., 92. 29.

Sadly means urgently, of heavy pressing necessity. "It *sadly* wants mendin."

Sag, to bend; to droop; having slackness.

Clothes-lines, telegraph-wires, &c., which are not tight, are said to *Sag*.

Sang, a song.

"Osanna king! to þe we cri
A sang." Curs. Mun., 15,049.

Scrat, scratch.

"*Scrat* her ees oot, Molly ; or else she 'll rahve thi hair."

> " And wit *skratting* he toke þe skurf
> He barked ouer as a turfe." Curs. Mun., 11,823.

Scrudged, crowded ; squeezed.

"We wer seeah *scrudged* up, we cud hardlins stor."

> " And then atweene her lilly handes twaine,
> Into his wound the juice therefore did *scruze*."
>
> F. Q., 3. 5. 33.

Seer, sure ; confident. A contraction of *seker* ; as *sure* is. a contraction of *secure.*

" Ah 's as *seer* on 't as Ah is o' standin here."

> " For þat is euer mare a *sekyr* standard
> þat will noghte (not) faile." Pr. Tr., 40.

Settle, a bench with a high back. Connected with *sit* and *seat.*

" He sat on yal-hoose *lang-settle* an dhrunk yal, whahl they tonned him oot."

"Opon the *setil* of his mageste." Pr. of Con., 6,122.

"To sitte in *setlis*." Curs. Mun., 18,997.

Shaav, or **Shiv,** or **Shav,** (Ice., skifa), a slice ; a piece cut, as of wheat, &c.

"It is safe taking a *shive* from a cut loaf."

Shanks, ankles ; legs.

"Is tha gannin ti ride? Ay, uppa *shanks* meear (mare)." (upon my own legs).

"Noo then ! sparra *shanks* (thin legs) get oot o' gate !"

> " He broken armes, he broken knes,
> He broken *shanks*, he broken thes " (thighs).
>
> Havelok, 1,901.

Sike, such.

"There was *sike* a row as Ah nivver heead afooar."

> " Puft up in pryde, *sik* as wes neuer sene
> Before, with ony mortall mannis eine." Lauder, 16. 422.

Sile, (Ice., sia) (1) to strain milk.

(2) A small wooden bowl, with a large aperture at the bottom, across which a piece of muslin is stretched, for the purpose of straining milk. This piece of muslin is the "*sile* cloot.*"

"Mary, is milk siled?" "Nooa!" "Then reeach ma *sile*, an Ah'll *sile* it."

(3) To faint, or glide away.

"Ghooast com clooase ti bedsteead, and began luggin at happin. It teeak twilt an pitcht it ower feeat-booad, then blankits, an wad ha thrawn sheet anole, bud Ah stuck tiv it; an when sumbody spak i' next rum ghooast *siled* away, an Ah nivver seed it ageean."

Skail, to scatter; to spill.

"Deean't *skail* sthreea (straw) aboot seeah."

"þai þat war *scaild* (scattered)." Curs. Mun., 19,505.

"He fetched out his bottle (bundle) and *scaled* the hay aboute."   Best, 78.

Skep, (Ice., skeppa) (1) a measure; as, a bushel *skep*; a peck *skep*.

(2) A wicker basket.

"Of his mete *scip*, (literally, bread-basket, stomach), was
      mesur nan, (none).
He wold ete seuen scep (sheep) him an."

                             Curs. Mun., 7453.

Skrike, (Ice., skrikja) to shriek; to scream.

"The little babe did loudly *scrike* and squall."

                         F. Q., Bk., 6., c. 5.

Slack, (Ice., slakki, a valley), a shallow valley. Common as a place name; *e.g.*, Nafferton Slack, Garton Slack, &c.

Slaver, (Ice., slafra), to run at the mouth with saliva. Also figuratively, meaning foul-mouthed, obscene; while, as *slaverment* it means fulsome flattery.

"And as she spake therewith she *slavered*."

                         F. Q., Bk. 5., c. 12.

F

Smatch, (Ice., smakka), a flavour or taste.   Wicliffe uses the older form—*smack.*

"He has some *smatch* of a Scholler."

Earle's Mic., (an Aturney).

Smoot, (Ice., smátt), a way or track.   Nearly obsolete, and applied only to the "run" of hares and rabbits.

"Leavinge an open *smoute* for them to go in." Best, 62.

Snape, (Ice., snape, a pert youth), to check; to correct; to snub.

"Ah sud *snape* that bayne, if Ah was thoo.   He's ower mich of his awn way."

 The Curs. Mun., 13,027, uses this word as meaning to accuse, to snub. "He com to *snaip* þe·king of sin."

Snitch, the nose.   With this word, we have connected, snipe (the bird with a long bill) snivel, snore, snort, snot (mucus) snout, sniff, snuff.

"The *snyte* (snipe) and the crowe shul dwell in it."

Wic., Is. 34. 11.

"Also tongis to do out the *snottis* (snuffs)."

Wic., Ex., 25. 38.

"Blaw thi *snitch*, an deean't sniffle like that."

Spell, a splinter of wood; a bar of wood.

The bars of a gate, ladder, chair, &c., are called *spells.*

"Ah've getten a *spell* i' mi finger."

"On which if a man lenith, it schal be brokun, and the *speel* thereof schal entre in hys hond."

Wic., 4 Kings, (2 Chron). 18. 21.

Spigot, a vent peg, inserted in beer barrels, &c.

"It is as must (new wine) without *spigot.*"

Wic., Job, 32. 19.

Spok or **Spak,** p.t. of to speak.

"Jesus *spac* to the peple." Wic., Matt., 23. 1.

Stacker, (Ice., stakra) to stagger; to bewilder.

"Weel, that reglar *stackers* ma!"

"For scho may *stakir* in þe strete." York Pl., 274. 85.

Stang, a pole or bar.

Riding the *stang* is a nearly-obsolete custom.

" A wicked iuu (Jew) wid wicked wrang
  Smate him wid a walker *stang.*
  þat he him brac his harn (brain) panne."

Curs. Mun., 21. 143.

Start, tail.   Obsolete, save in the name of a bird; the redstart.

"He dragged dust wiδ his *stert.*   Eng. Mis., 1. 9.

Steck or **Stike,** to fasten a gate or door.

Doors in old houses and churches are still fastened by a *stake* or bar; so "*stike* that deer," means fasten the door with a stake.

" He (Noah) self þe dore þan has he *stoken.*"

Curs. Mun., 1758.

" þe dores *stoke.*"   Curs. Mun., 19,313.

Stee, (Ice. *stegi*), a ladder.

This word is connected with step, steep, stair, stile (a little *stee*), and stirrup (a *stee* rope).

" He sette his foot in the *styrop* (stirrup)." Gamelyn, 189.

"He *stied* (mounted) into the boot (boat)."

Wic., Matt., 14. 32.

The sloping piece of wood by which fowls reach their roosting place is termed a hen-*stee.*

Sthrake, past tense of " to strike;" struck.

" He *sthrake* at rezzil (weasel) bud missed it."

" *Strake* on a rock, that under water lay,
  And perished past all recoverie."

Spenser (Visions of Petrarch) 2. 9.

Sthrang, strong.

" Bill's as *sthrang* as *sthrang* can be."

" For luf es *strang* als dede " (as death).   Pr. Tr., 2. 4.

Stiddy or **Stithy,** a blacksmith's anvil,

" Als (as) it war dintes (strokes) on a steþi
þat smithes smittes in a smeþey."

Curs. Mun., 23,237.

" As the *stithie* of an hamer betere." Wic., Job, 41. 15.

Storr or **Stower**, a heavy stick.

. " He beat her wi neeather stick, steean, iron, nor *stower*.

(Riding the Stang).

" The wright to come and putte in *stowers*." Best, 35.

Swad, a pod of peas, beans, &c.

The Authorised Version (Luke, 2. 12.) preserves a relative
of this word *swaddling* clothes.

· " Ah chuckt (threw) all peeah *swads* ti pigs."

Swap, to exchange ; to barter.

" Tom *swapt* ma knives, an ga ma a buttherie gun inti
bahgan."

. " The(y) *swapte* [blows] together tyll the(y) both swat."

Per. Rel., 43.

Swill, (1) to wash, by a drenching flood of water.

" *Swill* them flags !"

" Ful wel kan ich (I) dishes *swilen*." Havelok, 919.

(2) to swallow greedily. An immoderate drinker is said
to " *swill* it intiv him."

We have also the compounds, *swill*-tub, a tub for holding
swill (pig's food) ; and *swill*-kite, one who makes his kite
(stomach) a receptacle for *swill*—unnecessary liquids.

A humourous story relates how a cat " dhroondid hersen
i' *swill* tub, 'cos misthris had getten anuther cat."

Tally, (1) an account ; a score.

" Thoo mun keep *tally*."

(2) to match.

" What's tha browt theeas for ? They deean't *tally*."

(3) to agree ; to hold the same opinions.

" Ay ! they call mah wife *Tally*. Thoo sees oor feelins
tallied."

Teeam, to pour out.

"Ay, lass! Ah's riddy fo mi teeah ; *teeam* uz sum oot."
"The whilk (which) says *temys, temys.*" Psalter, 136. 10.
Thrapse, to trudge about.

An old woman, on her death-bed, was asked to take a
message to a previously-deceased person, when she sharply
replied, "Di ya think Ah sall he' nowt ti deeah i' heaven
bud gan *thrapsin* aboot, latein (searching) for hor?"

Threeap, to argue obstinately ; to dispute.
"Sha *threeapt* ma doon it was seeah."

    "Witvten þ*rep* or strijf
    Ai til (to) þe ending of þair lijf (life)."

                        Curs. Mun., 13,310.

"þan was þer no þ*repyng.*"   York Pl., 430. 105.

Tent, to tend ; to give heed to.

The person who tends pigs, cows, or birds is a pig-*tenther*,
coo-*tenther*, or bod-*tenther*, as the case may be.

"Eve! to me take *tent.*"   York Pl., 23. 41.

"þou will noghte *tente* to them."   Pr. Tr., p. 28.

Thrang, throng ; busy.

"Men was as *thrang* as could be."

"Who makis here all þis þ*rang*?"   York Pl., 178. 2.

Thof, though. The dialect has thruf for through ; pleeaf
for plough ; slafther for slaughter.

"*Thofe* I ware schreuen (shriven), me wanted contrycyone
(contrition)."   Pr. Tr. 7.

Three thrums, the purring of a cat. Thrumming is produced by tapping gently with the finger ends. Three thrums
is thrumming on a three (tree), a piece of wood, by which
process a good representation of the purring of a cat can be
obtained.

"Ah like ti hoar oor cat sing *three thrums.*"

Threed, thread.

"Gan ti Johnson shop an fetch a hank o' whitey-broon
threed."

"Take a nedyl and a þrede, and sewe þe fore partye to

þe after parti."   Ck. Bk. 40. 4.

Tickle, delicate ; ready to fall, go off, &c.

"It's a *ticklish* job is settin a thrap, seeah as ti leeave it *tickle*."

"On thing so *tickle* as th' unsteady ayre. F.Q., Bk. 7. c. 7.

" In humble dales is footing fast
• The trode is not so *tickle*." Sh. Cal. (July).

Tooan, or **Teean,** the one, (tuther, the other).

"þe *tane* es to þe toþer like."   Curs. Mun., 18,861.

"The fyrste es needfull us to do, the *tothire* we awe (ought) to do."   Pr. Tr., p. 10.

" He schal hate the *toon* and loue the *tother*."
                                        Wic., Matt., 6. 24.

Tundher, (Ice. tundr), tinder.

Once used with flint, steel, and brimstone matches to procure a light.

" Of ston mid stel (with steel) in ðe *tunder* " (they make a fire to) "warmen hem wel and heten and drinken."
                                        Old Eng. Mis., 17. 535.

Tree, wood.

Just as the word " wood " means a quantity of living trees as well as a piece of a dead tree, so the word " tree " has two similar meanings—a living tree, and anything made of the tree after it is felled.   Thus we have cross-*tree* (cross bits of wood); boot-*tree* (a wooden implement used by a shoemaker for Wellington boots); axle-*tree* ; roof-*tree* ; rig-(roof) *tree* ; gallows-*tree* ; swingle-*tree* (the swinging wood to which horses are yoked); cobble-*tree*, or kibble-*tree* (the coupling wood, by which two horses are yoked abreast); maisther-*tree* (the master or chief yoking beam, by which four horses can be yoked abreast, sometimes called a fower-hoss balk).

" A man com til (to) him, and bedd (bade)
    He suld him mak a *treen* bedd." Curs. Mun., 12,391.

"As ded as a dore *tree*."   P. P., I., 185.

"An putte al in a fayre *treen* bolle " (wooden bowl).

Ck. Bk., 16.

Ugly, horrible; dreadful.

"That's a *ugly* spot ti drahve past on a dahk neet."

" *Vgly* it is to fall in there hend." Psal., 9. 37.

Wahk, to ache; ache or pain.

Thus we have heead-*wahk* (head-ache); teeath-*wahk*; ear-*wahk*; belly-*wahk*; &c.

"Abouen (above) the *warkynge* of thaire woundes."

Psalter, 243. 68.

"Than ar thai sek ore thar hed *werkis*."—*Then are they sick, or their head aches.* R. R., 86. 352.

Wahk, work.

"Helpe, lady Werburge, this *warke* to amende."

St. Werb., 1,212.

"Thou fulfillis in *warke* that thow es called in name."

Pr. Tr., 1.

"And buildest strong *warke* upon a weake ground."

Sh. Cal., (May).

Waffin, wafting; waving. Connected with *weave, weft.*

"Deean't *waff* aboot seeah! Sit thi-sen doon!"

"The Iustice and the scherreue bothe honged hye,
To weyuen (shake, waff) with the ropes and with the
wynde drye." Gam. 880.

Wakken, to awake.

"Wakken up, thoo greeat sleepy heead!"

"It es time for to *wacken* him." Curs. Mun., 14200.

Wankle, unsteady; unstable.

"Tom's been badly (ill) seeah lang, whahl he's varry *wankle* noo."

"ᛞis wunder woneᛞ (dwells)
in *wankel* stede. (insecure places)."

Eng. Mis., 18. 566.

Waykly, or **Wayk,** weak, delicate.

"He was awlas a *waykly* bayn."

" Full *wayke* I was." York Pl., 43. 93.

" ʒe skar the *wayklings* from the wourd (scripture)."

Lauder, 16. 414.

"Scho wexe *wayke* (grew weak) and sodanly all was
awaye." Pr. Tr., 6.

Wax, to grow.

A growing child is said to be *waxin*, and *waxin* pains are
growing pains

" Whereat he gan to *wex* exceeding wroth."

F. Q., Bk. 3. c. 9.

Wesan or **Weeasan**, the wind-pipe.

" Had his *wesand* bene a little widder." Sh. Cal., (Sep.)

Wem, (Ice., vamm), a spot; a mole (dark-coloured spot).

"Maiden ber barn witvten *wemme* (bore child without
spot)." Curs., Mun., 11,226.

" Of all vertus withowttyne *weme* of synn." Pr. Tr., 38.

Whom, home.

" They escaped all daunger.

Cam *whom* safe and sonde." St. Werb., 1,808.

" To offre to the (thee) a gyfte at my comyng *whome*."

St. Werb., 1464.

" At his *whom* comyng to Englande
from Normandy." St. Werb., 1. 541.

In the different parts of the Riding the word *home* becomes
hooam, heeam, wom, yam, &c.

Wrate, p. t. of to write.

"Thou *wrate* it in my herte." Psalter, 426. 102.

Yat, (A.-S., geat; Middle Eng., yate), a gate.

"Shut that *yat*, an ton (turn) that coo (cow)."

" For at þe ute-cuming o þe *yatte*
He turnd again." Curs. Mun., 12,593.

ADDITIONAL SPECIMENS OF THE DIALECT.

Rooads is despad sluthery, bud it's dhry aboon heead.
Jim an me's rayther across just noo.
Ah's varry tired; Ah've been afeeat all day.
Ah can beeat him all ti nowt at walkin.
Awd man gets ti gan varry mitch astoop.   He's awdened a vast leeatly.
Bob's getten a pair o' bellas'd beeats this back end.
Noo, then! Bessy-babs! thoo's gennin ageean.
Bayn kept his-sen quiet bi blawin blebs.
Thay all fell uppa yan anuther, bud Bill was boddom-most.
Thoo's a bonny honey ti sthrike at thi awn fayther.

> We had a pie, meead o' rye,
>   An stinkin was all meeat;
> It was sa teeaf, we had aneeaf,
>   An mare then we could eeat.

Biggest breet Ah knaw aboot was yah hahvist.   Watther started ti cum doon dhreean efther teeah, an whon Ah gat up aboot midneet, middas was all breet.   Ah called all lads up, an we fetched sheep yam i' cahts an waggins.
We're gannin ti put Billy inti button cleeas o' Sunda.
This job owt ti be deean ti-neet, bi reets.
Machine lewks capadosha; an sha gans capadosha.

Fooaks sez he's rich; bud there wad be nowt left, if he was cindhered up.

> Mah awd granmother, she is deead,
> She lane't ma hoo ti mak cockelty breead;
> It's up wi yer heels an doon wi yer heead.
> An that's oor way ti mak cockelty breead.

An seeah y'u call all yon threes wiv all yon craw nests in a craw-shaw; bud iv oor toon we used ti call em a craw-wood, or else a craw-beeld.

Cum thi ways, mah bayn, an give az a kiss.

Ay, sha's a good-fo'-nowt; sha stands ommast all day i' frunt deear-steead.

New fooaks browt sike a dollop o' stuff wiv em.

He fiddled an faddled aboot seeah whahl Ah was sick o' seein him.

Is it a frost ti-neet? Hey! a duck-frost!

Ah fell full smack o' mi feeace.

Hey, Ah want a wife; bud Ah deean't want neean o' yer booadin-skeeal lasses, at plays pianners an sike like. Ah want yan at can milk ky, fodher-up hosses, an muck-oot pig-sties. Ah want a useful beeast."

He's a rare dab hand at his wahk, if he is gallic-handed.

It's hard cheese when yan o' yan awn bayns tons ther backs o' yan.

Poor awd Mally! sha's had nowt bud hard-sailin all her life-tahm.

What a hawvy-gawvy Sammy-Codlin sooat ov a chap oor Jack is.

> Squint-ee squinny,
> Sell'd his ee for a guinea,
> When he gat heeam, guinea was bad,
> An seeah poor Squint-ee squinny ran mad.

When oor wagginer gets on ti yal-hoose lang-settle, he'll sit a awd hen-sit.

If thoo's cum'd iv a quahther ov a noor, thoo's cum'd hie-tha-rally.

> A greeat hobble-de-hoy,
> 'Twixt a man an a boy.

Noo, deean't let it cum doon wiv a soss; humour it doon.

Thof he hez deean badly bi me, Ah wadn't deeah him a ill-ton.

Wimmin weears ther goons si lang noo-a-days, at they gan lallapin ivver si far uppa grund.

Cum leetly, gan leetly, Ah gat tha wi mi wife. (Said of one who squanders his wife's fortune).

Thoo hez it ti deeah, an if tha dizzn't like it, thoo may lump it.

Ah ! y'u'll get nowt oot ov him. He's a narra-chined an.

She's nattherinest awd woman Ah ivver seed; she's ommast natthered her chine away.

Thoo'd needlins be shamm'd o' thi-sen, ti talk like that.

Bob's a reglar nivver-sweeat; he's awlas lewkin oot all ways fo' Sundas.

Oor fooaks is undher-handed rayther then ower-handed, bud they'll mannish amang hands.

Jack's a sthrange pafty chap.

There's ower mich fo' yan, an scarcelins aneeaf fo' tweeah.

> Here we are as tite as nip,
> We nivver flang ower bud yance iv a grip,
> Grip was sa wahd, at we cudn't sthrahd,
> An seeah we cum yam wi looad ov a sahd.

[Another version of the Harvest Song, p. 12. Here follow two versions of the second verse].

> We've rovven oor shets, we've torn wer skin,
> Ti get this merry hahvist in ;
> An noo we've getten it tightly stackt.
> We mun set ti wahk, an hev it thackt.

Ah 've rovven mi shet, an torn mi skin,
Ti get mi maisther hahvest in.
Hahvist in an hahvist oot,
We 've bet all fahmers roond aboot.

That scheeam o' them chaps was all a suck-in.   Ah knaw it, for Ah was suckt in.

Ah 's tired oot o' sitting here, wivoot a bit o' back-hod.

Deean't gan an bemeean thi-sen bi gannin wiv hor.

Children cry out to the bat, flitting above their heads, "Bat, bat, cum undher mi hat," and throw their caps up in the air to catch the creature.   In some places they say,

" Black, black beear-away,
Cum doon bi here-away."

Thing lewkt weel aneef ti staht wiv; bud what a bloit it ended wiv.

Mah neck is sare, 'cos collar 's fridged it all day lang.

Ratten just ga three ficks, and then it deed.

He legged ma doon wi gib end ov his stick.

There 's a pluke cummin upov his aym, at 's bad ti like.

Jack 's best-like bayn i' all famly.

We 've had a varry blustherous day, bud it 's a varry lownd neet.

It 's a sowmy neet; Ah 's ommast mafted.

Bob was pawky, an seeah Ah gav him yan ower his smeller.

It 's all askew, like oor Mally mooth.

Thoo says reet; he is sthrang i' aym, bud he 's wake i' brain.

Sun was bleeazin yat yisthada, an summer-colt was oot all day lang.

Whah, Ah 'll be shoggin on, an thoo 'll owertak ma.

Noo thrig thi weeam, an deean't cum yam hungry.

Ah went ti see what sooat o' things he 'd getten, bud sike a van-jotthery Ah nivver seed afooar.

Deean't jowp coffee-pot an stor all gruns up.

Let's ram away, an get job deean.

Ah's as full as a tick; Ah've had sike a jawtheram o' broth.

Diz tha think Ah's gannin ti be domineered ower wiv a wackey like thoo.

Bonny is at bonny diz.

Bayn hez belly-wahk wi cranshin si mich rewbub.

He's aboot dawziest chap Ah ivver seed.

Ey! Ah've getten it sahtanly, bud nobbut bi dhribs an dhrabs.

What's matther, Bill? Matther! Whah, yon dizzy-heeaded feeal's teean mah dikin-beeats, an cutten tops up ti mend bahfin wiv.

When we led wheeat, it dozz'd oot a seet ti be seen.

Ay, bayn! what a lahtle fat dabs thoo is.

Sha just tawmed ower, an siled doon, an if Ah hadn't clickt hod'n her, sha wad he' tummeld inti fire.

When a child's tooth comes out, it must be dropped into the fire, and the following rhyme said, or the child will have to seek its tooth after death:

> "Fire, fire, tak a beean,
> An send oor Johnny a good teeath ageean."

I' summer tahm, Ah likes ti sit wi thruf-oppen deears, an get a nice breeze.

Tom-feeals diz Tom-feeal things.

He was bad afooar, bud he's wahse-like noo.

Cum on, an Ah'll fight all web o' ya.

Awd machine wants fitlin up waintly.

Thoo didn't cum ti see uz las neet! What gat tha?

If ya say Oor Fayther (the Lord's Prayer) wrang-ways on, tha divvel 'll cum.

He dhrank a pahnt o' yal, all at yah slowp, wivoot a yottan,

Ah can beleeave meeast o' what thoo's telled ma, bud Ah's seer thoo's wraxin noo.

> Ah set mi back ageean a yat,
> Thinkin it wor a thrusty three,
> Bud stowp it bent, an then it brak,
> An sike was mah threw luv ti me.

(Fragment of a song).

Shut thi gob, thoo dafty whatty, an deean't talk sike baldherdash.

Tak skeel, an gan an milk ky.

That hoose must he' teean a weight o' brass ti beeld.

Thoo nobbut lewks varry wawey this mooanin! What's matther wi tha? Whah, Ah's nobbut midlin!

> If ya saw him bud walk, you would laugh fit ti brust,
> For tooan leg or tuther is seer ti be fust.

When he tell'd ma there was fooaks at tuther sahd o' yath, wi ther feet tiv oor's, it stummled ma ti knaw hoo it was they didn't tummle off.

Thoo's nobbut been ti chotch fower tahms i' thi life :— when thi fayther deed, when thi muther deed, when thoo was kessened, an when thoo was wed.

Let's bon all this awd toffer, an mak a bit mare rum.

Ah ken it biv ee-seet, bud Ah deean't knaw it neeam,— said a school-boy of a certain letter, when learning his alphabet.

He chunthered fo' lang aneeaf, just 'cos he cudn't deeah what he liked.

He had ti clame wall ower wi tar, an he clamed his-sen anole, an neeah mistak.

Whah, that caps Leatherstarn, and Leatherstarn capped the divvel.

It's a varry chollus wind this mooanin.

Think on an tell blacksmith ti get mah cowlrake deean bi ti-mooan.

Think me on ti get sum fire-eldin in te-neet.

Whah, sitha! that conny lahtle bayn can run aboot like a two-year-awd (horse).

Frumaty an rice wants weel creein, or else it isn't nice.

Pump swape 's brokken, an we he' ni watther.

What a cluntherin thoo maks, when thoo gans across fleear.

It 's nobbut a bit o' cleean muck, at weean't hot neeahbody.

Cum thi ways, mah bayn, an let 's noss tha.

What a lahtle doit of a fella he is.

Bayns croodled tegither, an kept ther-sens wahm.

What a tan-tawdherly woman Bess Robbison is.

Jack 's as good as his maisther.

It 's a good bit sin Ah was there, bud when Ah went a goodish few fooaks went anole.

Thoo can't hod on lang at that bat.

They 're flaid o' cholera, an seeah bellman 's cried herrins doon.

Bacon swarth was all cothered up, an as hahd as a steean.

Mah stockin had all ruckt up i mi beeat, an raised a bleb o' mi heel.

Oor Dick was flaid o' gannin intiv ooachad las' neet; he sed Awd Goggie wad get him.

She was iv a hig, 'cos Ah wadn't lether hev her new bonnit on.

They 're two reglar scally-brats, an went at it hoothoo-an-noothoo for a noor an mare.

Las' Kesmas, we had ice-cannles a yahd lang, hingin fre' spoot end.

Ah thried mi best ti insense it intiv him, an yet Ah cudn't mak him undherstand it.

> Oud bless the maysther of this hoose,
>   The mistheriss also;
> An all the little intepunks,
>   That round your table go.

(Stanza of the Christmas Carol of the Vessle-cup women).

Joggle his memory for him!

Whah, thrain's geean! Sha was seeah lang getting her fal-lals on, an smartenin her-sen up, at Ah thowt we sud be lanted, an Ah's reet.

It was twenty year last Cannlemas sin yoor greeat awm three blew doon; bud Ah mind it like as agif it was nobbut yisthada.

He said Ah sud nivver win if Ah bet o' Sundas; an Ah said sahtanly yan on az mun win, an that nailed him.

He's aboot deean for. He gans pottherin aboot shop, bud can't deeah nowt good for owt.

Ah thowt ther wad he' been summat left, bud ther wahnt a skorrick.

Gan an wesh thi-sen; thi hans is set in wi muck.

Sha cums oot o' Sundas iv all her fahn toggery.

Noo then! What's tha sidelin up ti ma for? Ah knaw thoo wants summat.

Diz tha think Ah's boon ti dhrink sike slappy stuff as that teeah? No! that Ah weean't!

Bayn taks efther his fayther.

Bessey braids ov her muther.

Days begins ti tak-off noo.

Awd Sally's a reg'lar awd genny-gibs.

That was as near as a toucher.

Noo! what's tha think ti that? Isn't that a topper?

lt's fotty year, cum Kesmas, sin me an mah awd deeam was wed.

Jack rolled doon hill, an towpled ower-tail.

Such expressions as these could be greatly multiplied, but they must suffice as Specimens.

BIBLIOGRAPHY OF WORKS

RELATING TO THE DIALECT OF THE EAST RIDING OF YORKSHIRE.

COMPILED BY W. G. B. PAGE,

Sub-Librarian, Subscription Library, Hull.

BROWNE, REV. THOMAS, of Kingston-upon-Hull. Poems on Several Occasions. Printed for Vernòr and Hood, London, and sold by Merritt and Wright, Liverpool, and Thomas Browne, Hull. 1800. 8vo. pp. xxviii. 179.

[On pp. 151-166, there are several "Specimens of the Yorkshire Dialect." Mr. Browne, though born at Lastingham, was educated at the Hull Grammar School. Editor of the *Hull Advertiser*, in 1797, for which paper he wrote some dialect poems and dialogues under the *nom de plume* of "Alexis."]

"BYRONICA." (Edward Wade, a native of Tollerton, and a seaman on one of Wilson's ships.

Oor Sammy. *Hull Bellman*, vol. vi. (4th Sep., 1880), p. 11.

Gooarge Herrysmith's Neetmeeare. *Hull Bellman*, vol. vi. (20th Nov., 1880), p. 5.

Laatle Loois. *Hull Bellman*, vol. vi. (16th Oct., 1880), p. 7.

Taailor Herrysmith's Giblet Pie. *Hull Bellman*, vol. vi. (30th Oct., 1880), p. 11.

[None of "Byronica's" pieces are pure East Riding. The influence of the North Riding is strong.]

G

COLE, REV. E. MAULE, M.A., Vicar of Wetwang, Yorkshire.
Scandinavian Place Names in the East Riding of
Yorkshire. (with dialect) 8vo.

Countryman's Story, The. From the "Hull Bazaar Gazette."
Hull Advertiser, April 25th, 1863.
[A story in seven verses, which was written for the Hull Rifle
Bazaar.]

ENGLISH DIALECT SOCIETY.
Glossary, A, of Words used in Holderness in the East
Riding of Yorkshire, by Frederick Ross, F.R.H.S.,
Richard Stead, F.R.H.S., and Thomas Holderness.
London: Published for the English Dialect Society,
by Trübner and Co. 8vo. pp. v. 162.
[Being "Series C. Original Glossaries and Glossaries with fresh
additions," of the publications of the Dialect Society.]

Glossary of North of England Words, by J. H.
Five Glossaries by Mr. Marshall, namely: East
Yorkshire, East Norfolk, the Vale of Gloucester,
the Midland Counties, and West Devonshire, and
a West Riding Glossary, by Dr. Willan, Edited by
Rev. W. W. Skeat. 1873. 8vo.

Glossaries, five re-printed, including Wiltshire, East
Anglian, Suffolk, and East Yorkshire Words, and
Dialectical Words from Bishop Kenneth's Parochial
Antiquities, Edited by the Rev. Prof. Skeat, M.A.
English Dialect Society. 1879. 8vo.

HAMILTON, REV. RICHARD WINTER, Minister of Belgrave
Chapel, Leeds.

Nugæ Literaria : Prose and Verse. London : Hamilton, Adams, and Co. ; Smith, Elder, and Co. ; and
Jackson and Walford. Leeds: J. Y. Knight, and
John Cross. 1841. 8vo. viii. 586 pp.
[On pp. 289-364, there is an exhaustive chapter "On the Yorkshire Dialect" generally, which gives an illustrative glossary of
words and their derivations.]

HOLDERNESS, THOMAS, editor of the *Driffield Observer* and joint-author of "A Glossary of Words used in Holderness in the East Riding of Yorkshire."

Some Place-Names of the East Riding of Yorkshire. Driffield : Printed at the office of the *Driffield Observer.* 1881. 8vo. 32 pp.

Specimens of the Yorkshire Dialect, as spoken in the East Riding of the County, and more particularly in the North-Eastern portion of the Riding, with a copious Glossary. Driffield : Printed and published by T. Holderness. 1887. 8vo. 48 pp.

See also "Holderness Glossary."

LANCASTER, GEORGE, Hull.

Stringy Pie : a Yorkshire Ditty. By "Killpudding." *Hull Bellman,* vol. vi. (4th Sep., 1880), p. 7.

A Yorkshire Story. By Spring Bank, Esquire, Gentleman. In thirteen chapters.

[This story, which appeared weekly in the *Hull Critic,* from May 19th to August 4th, contains a number of East Riding Dialect Words.]

Schoolmaster and his Visitors, The : a Poem. "Lays and Lyrics." Hull, 1880. pp. 33 to 40.

Cockney Critic, The : a Poem. By C. W. Soderquist.

Tommy Sharp in the Country : a Chapter from the Records of the Hull Children's Holiday Fund.

[This is a long Poem, in which are introduced many well-known Yorkshire sayings.]

Ishmael's Prayer : a bit of East Riding Dialect. *Hull Arrow,* Feb. 23rd, 1889, p. 11.

[Giving an account of the mode of praying adopted by a half-witted farmer's son, who resided in the neighbourhood of Hull.]

STEAD, RICHARD, F.R.H.S.

Holderness and the Holdernessians : a Few Facts on the History, Topography, Dialect, Manners and

Customs of the District : by a Fellow of the Royal
Historical Society.   London : Trübner and Co.,
Broadway, Ludgate Hill.   Hull : William Hunt,
42, Whitefriargate. 1878. 8vo. 121 pp. appendix
vi. pp.

Holderness Words of a Fighting Character. *Leisure
Hour*, Feb. 1879, p. 75.

See also "Holderness Glossary."

THOMPSON, THOMAS, F.S.A., Welton.

Researches into the History of Welton and its Neighbourhood : with a few remarks, chiefly of an Antiquarian Nature, about some Adjacent Places in
Yorkshire, and about the Yorkshire Language.
Printed for private circulation amongst his friends
and neighbours.   Kingston-upon-Hull : J. W.
Leng, 15, Savile Street. 8vo. pp. vi. 205.

[The Second Part, pp. 107-196, the "Neighbourhood of Welton
and the Surrounding Districts," contains a large number of dialect
words and their origin.]

WILSON, ISAAC, bookseller, Hull, and printer and publisher
of *The Hull Advertiser*.

The Country Politicians : or Joahney and Tommy.
A Dialogue in the Yorkshire Dialect, by "Apedale"
Hull Advertiser, April 20th, 1799.

Yorkshire Dialect, The, Exemplified in various Dialogues,
Tales, and Songs, applicable to the County.
To which is added a Glossary of such words
as are likely not to be understood by those unac-
quainted with the Dialect.   London : John Russell
Smith, 4, Old Compton Street, Soho Square.
1839. 8vo. 24pp.

[This is a similar selection to Mr. Holderness' "Specimens," and
contains contributions by the late Rev. Thomas Browne, Hull, and
D. Lewis.]

GLOSSARIAL INDEX.

Athof, though ; as though, 36.

Attercop, 50.

Awdened, aged, 89.

Awd Nooah, 5.

Awlas, always, 91.

Awm three, elm tree, 96.

Axe, 50.

Back-end, latter part of the year, 89.

Backer-end, 50.

Back-hod, a hold or rest for the back, 92.

Bad, did bid, 36.

Bad-ti-like, bad-looking, 92.

Bahfin, horse collar, 93.

Bahgeeast, 32. 33. 50.

Balk, 51.

Ballocks, 51.

Balderdash, foolish talk, 94.

Band, 51.

Baste, 51.

Bat, rate ; speed, 95.

Bate, 51.

Bawmy, simpleton, 32.

Bayn, 42. 51. 52. 90.

Bazzacked, flogged, 40.

Beald, 52.

Beck, 3. 6. 52.

Beeal, 3. 32. 38. 52.

Bellas'd beeats, boots having the tongues sewn to the uppers, 89.

Beldher, 52.

Belly-wabk, 52.

Belltinker, 23. 41.

Bemeean, disgrace, 92.

Bent, determined, 52.

Besom, 52.

Bessy-babs, a child who cries for little cause, 89.

Best-like, best-looking, 92.

Bested, got the better of, 36.

Beughs, 52.

Bile, 53.

Billy, hat, 38.

Bi reets, by rights, 89.

Bink, 53.

Blared, bellowed ; roared, 33.

Blash, 53.

Blathery, wet; muddy, 33. 53.

Blebs, bubbles ; blisters, 89. 95.

Bloit, failure; miscarriage, 92.

Blustherous, windy ; stormy, 92.

Bluther, 53.

Boak, to balk ; to thwart, 42.

Boggle, 33. 53.

Bole, 54.

Bolt, 52.

Bonny-honey, a nice sweet thing (said with contempt). 89.

Boon, 53.

Botch, 54.

Boult, 53.

Braids, grows like, 96.

Brant, 17.

Brass, 34. 54. 94.

Brazzocks, 54.

Breed, 54.

Breet, a flood ; flooded, 89.

Brig, 36, 55.

Broc, 55.

Brogues, 55.

Brust, 55.

Brussen, 29.

Bug, 17.

Bullace, 17.

Bunch, 24, 55.

Busk, 55.
Byre, cow house, 45.
Caff, 56.
Caffle, noisy talk, 39.
Callit, 56.
Callitin-boot, 24.
Cap, 56. 94.
Capadosha, grand, 89.
Cassan, 18.
Cassimere, a coarse material, 39.
Cawsey, causeway ; path, 32.
Chavel, 56.
Cheer, 56.
Childher, 56.
Chollus, bitterly cold, 94.
Chunthered, grumbled, 94.
Cindhered up, 90.
Clack, 56.
Clam, 2.
Clame, daub ; besmear, 94.
Clap, 25. 57.
Clart, 57.
Clew, 57.
Click, 57, 93.
Clooases, fields, 24. 36.
Cloot, (1) a patch, 57.
    (2) a blow, 25. 34.
Clooted, knocked, 24.
Cobble, 28. 58.
Cock, 58.
Cocklety breead, 90.
Cog up, treasure up, 42.
Collops, 58. 73.
Conny, little, 95.
Cool, 58.
Coshan, question, 68.
Cothered, puckered; wrinkled. 95.

Cowlrake, a rake for ashes, 40. 94.
Cranshin, crushing with the teeth, 93.
Cratch, 58.
Craw, 16. 49.
Crawshaw ; Craw-wood ; Craw-beeld ; a rookery, 90.
Creein, parboiling, 95.
Creeal, a strong wooden frame, 34.
Croodled, nestled, 95.
Croose, 17. 59.
Crud, 59.
Cummers and Ganners, visitors, 62.
Cutten, has cut, 93.
Dabs, a fat child, 93.
Dab-hand, 90.
Daft, 59. Compounds of, 3.
Dag, 58.
Dale, 59.
Dawziest, silliest, 93.
Deed, died, 94.
Deng, 25. 59.
Dess, 59.
Despad, desperately ; very, 24. 89.
Dhribs an dhrabs, bits; instalments, 93.
Dhrop, 25. 59.
Didher, 59.
Dike, 2. 33.
Dikin-beeats, ditching boots, with high tops, 83.
Dill, 60.
Din, 60.
Dodhered, 32. 60.
Dog-noper, 76.
Doit, a little thing, 95.

Dollup, a heap, 90.
Dooment, something to do; adventure, 34.
Dowills, 60.
Dowly, 4.
Dozzed oot, shook out, 93.
Duck frost, a shower of rain, 90.
Dumplîn, suet pudding, 20. 60.
Een, 60.
Ee-seet, eye-sight, 94.
Efther, 60.
Esh, ash, 26. 32.
Fan, did find; found, 33. 45.
Feeath, 61.
Fettle, 61.
Fey, 45. 61.
Ficks, convulsive kicks, 92.
Fiddled and Faddled, dawdled, 90.
Fire-fanged, 4.
Fire-eldin, fire-wood, 95.
Flaid, 33. 37. 51. 52. 61. 95.
Flit, 61.
Fog, 61.
Fond, 33. 61.
Fooar-elders, 62.
Fooar-dear, front door, 90.
Fodher, give fodder to, 90.
Fowt (1) did fight.
   (2) a fool; a simpleton, 45.
Fra, 62.
Framed, 75.
Freshwood, 62.
Fridged, chafed, 92.
Frumaty, porridge made of wheat, 95.
Frush, 62.
Full pelt, at full speed, 33.

Full smack, 62. 90.
Fullock, 34. 40. 62.
Fulth, 4. 62.
Fuzzack, a donkey, 33.
Gahth, 63.
Gain, 62.
Gainist, nearest, 33.
Galli-balk, 4.
Gallic-handed, left-handed, 90.
Gan, 62. 33. 93. 92.
Gat, got, 34. 93.
Gate, (1) way; road, 3. 63. 80.
   (2) right of pasture, 63.
   (3) manner, 36. 63.
Gaum, 63.
Gavlac, 43. 63. 77.
Geeas, tailor's iron, 33. 34.
Gen, 29. 63. 89. 96.
Genny-gibs, one always whining and crying, 96.
Getten, 4. 63.
Gib, hooked, 92.
Gif, if, 64.
Gift-i-gob, 64.
Glooar, 64.
Glowpin, 64.
Gob, 3. 27. 29. Compounds of, 4.
Golly, 64.
Gooaved, stared, 46.
Good bit sin, a long time since, 95.
Grape, 36. 65.
Grave, to dig, 64.
Greeas, 64.
Grip, 12. 64. 91.
Grov. 3.
Growsome, 4.
Grub, 64.

Grund, 3. 64.
Hack, 7. 65.
Haft, 65.
Hales, 34. 65.
Hansel, 65.
Hanted, 66.
Happin, 66. 81.
Hard, 66.
Hard cheese, hard to bear, 90.
Harden, 66.
Hardlins, hardly; scarcely, 36.
Hard salin, trouble; misfortune, 90.
Hask, 66.
Hawvy-gauvy, simple, foolish, 94.
Healthsome, healthful, 4.
Heead-wahk, head ache, 5.
Heeam, 6. 32. 33. 66.
Heeap, 66.
Hedgin-steeak, a stake used in making fences, 34.
Hen-sit, a long sitting, like that of a hen upon her eggs, 90.
Heppenest, smartest, 38.
Hick, 67.
Hickin-barra, 34. 67.
Hie-tha-rally, a quick pace, 91.
Hig, a fit of ill temper, 95.
Hing-lug, 4. 67.
Hooam, 6. 88.
Hopper, the funnel - shaped receptacle for corn, seeds, &c., in mills or machines, 39.
Hoothoo-an-Noothoo, first one and then the other, 95.
Hud, a ledge at the back of a fire-place, 16.
Hugged, carried, 36.

Humour, yield to; to steady, 91.
Ill-ton, ill turn, 91.
Inkle weeavers, 21.
Insense, to make clear too; to drive the sense of a matter into a person's mind, 95.
Intepunks, children, 95.
Jannack, a lump, 38.
Jawtheram, a large quantity, 92.
Jenny Oolat, an owl, 33.
Joan's Dyke, 32. 33.
Job, work, 33. 50. 75. 89.
Joggle, to remind, 96.
Jowl, 27. 67.
Jowp, shake; disturb, 92.
Kaff, chaff, 2.
Keeal pot, 35.
Kelther, Keltherment, rubbish; lumber, 35. 45.
Ken, churn, 46. 61.
Kep, 67.
Kesmas, Christmas, 96.
Kessened, christened, 94.
Kest, a cast; a squint, 38.
Kest, cast; throw, 67.
Kinnle, 68.
Kist, 2. 34. 35. 68.
Kitlin, 22. 68.
Kittle, delicate; sensitive, 19. 68.
Kittle, to tickle, 68.
Krake, 68.
Krewk, a crooked handle, 61.
Ky, cows, 90. 94.
Labber, daub; besmear, 41.
Laboursome, labourious, 4.
Lahm kill, lime kiln, 35. 78.

Lake, 28. 69. 70.
Lallapin, trailing, 91.
Lane, to teach, 69.
Lang settle, a long seat; a bench, 90.
Lanted, belated, 96.
Lap, 69.
Lasses, servants, 35.
Late, 69. 85.
Lathe, 69.
Lather, perspiration, 36.
Led, carted away, 93.
Lee, a lie, 2. 69.
Leeaced, 27. 38.
Leeath-wake, 69.
Leeav, 69.
Leet, 70.
Lig, 31. 35. 37. 41. 44. 70.
Like, look. See "Best like"; "Bad ti like."
Lin, 70.
Lit, did alight, 36.
Litha, 70.
Liver, to deliver, 70.
Lop, 5. 71.
Loup, 36. 71.
Louse, loose, 71.
Low, a flame, 71.
Lug (1) to carry, 46.
    (2) the ear, 5. 38.
Luggin, (1) carrying, 46.
    (2) pulling, 27. 81.
Lump it, submit to circumstances, 91.
Mafted, overcome with heat, 92.
Maisther, master, 3. 5. 92.
Mak, 72.
Malak, commotion, 32.
Mandhers, manners, 37.

Mang, 72.
Mare, more, 34. 72.
Maste, 73.
Mawk, 22.
Mawkin, image; effigy, 39. 41.
Mene, or Meny, 73.
Mense, 4. 73.
Messment, 4.
Middas, meadows, 89.
Middin, 36. 73.
Milt, 73.
Mind, a resolve, 74.
Mizzle, 74.
Moel, a spot, 74.
Mouther, 74.
Muck, 36. 74. 90. 95.
Mullock, 75.
Mun, must, 75.
Nailin, 28. 30. 96.
Narra-chined, niggardly, 91.
Natther, to complain; to grumble, 91.
Neeaf, 27. 40. 45. 75.
Needlins, of need; of necessity, 91.
Nivver-sweeat, one who is so idle, that he never sweats over his work, 91.
Nobbut, only, 94. 96.
Noddle, 75.
Nominy, 7.
Nope, 28. 75.
Norrayshun, 38. 41.
Nowt, nothing, 89.
Octoavers, large feet, 39.
Odd, single, 62.
Oddment, remnant, 4.
Offa, off from, 34. 76.
Offense, oft times; often, 33.

Ommast, almost, 32. 33. 35. 90.
Ooachad, orchard, 95.
Oor, 95.
Otther, 4. 46. 76.
Ower-handed, having more men than necessary, 91.
Owmly, 76.
Pafty, irritable; easily provoked, 91.
Pale or Pailins, 33. 76.
Pash, 20.
Pawk, 23. 77.
Pawky, impudent, 20, 30, 92.
Pet, offence, 77.
Pick, push, 28.
Pissimire, 34. 77.
Plantin, a plantation; a wood, 33.
Pluke, a little boil, 92.
Pooak, poke; sack, 5. 77.
Possessed, held, 77.
Potherin, doing anything in a slow, unskilful way, 96.
Powst, post, 23.
Pucker, 77.
Puddle, 77.
Purchass, 77.
Quick sticks, speedily, 24.
Quietsome, 77.
Rack-a-pelt, a scamp, 29.
Raggill, 77.
Rag-lad, 21.
Rag oot, temper; passion, 34.
Rake, 78.
Ram, strong; fœtid, 20.
Rame, 78.
Ram away, push ahead; work hard, 93.
Ramp, 78.

Ratten, a rat, 25. 46, 92.
Rawmed, sprawled, 33.
Reckons, hooks on which pans are hung, 4.
Reek, 35. 50.
Remmon, 78.
Rendher, to melt, 78.
Rensh, to rinse, 78.
Rezzil, a weasel, 20. 83.
Rig, 78.
Rigged, set up; prepared, 34.
Rock, 79.
Roosin, 79.
Rovven, torn, 92. 93. Rove, 24.
Ruck, to wrinkle; to gather in folds, 95.
Rudd, 20.
Ryme, hoar frost, 79.
Sad, heavy, 20. 79.
Sadly, urgently, 79.
Sag, 46. 79.
Sahk, sark; shirt; smock, 45.
Scally-brat, a scold; a virago, 95.
Scarcelins, scarcely, 91.
Scopperil, 22.
Scrat, 80.
Scrawmed, sprawled, 33.
Scrudged, 20. 80.
Seckaree, a short smock, 38.
Secks, sacks; bags, 34. 35.
Seer, sure, 80.
Settle, a bench, 80.
Shaav, or Shaff, 40. 80.
Shaffled, shuffled; walked in a slovenly manner, 32. 33.
Shoggin, going slowly.

Tally, 84.

Tan-tawdherly, tawdry ; slovenly, 95.

Tatie-trap, potátoe-trap (i.e. the mouth), 5.

Taties, potatoes, 23.

Tawmed, swooned, 93.

Teeam, 94.

Tent, 85.

Thareckly, directly, 29.

Theaker, 13.

Theakin, 50.

Thersens, themselves, 34.

Thrapse, 85.

Threed, 85.

Thrig thi weeam, fill thy stomach, 92.

Throppled, choked, 34.

Thruf oppen, open through-out, 93.

Thrussle, a trestle ; a support for a table, 34.

Tick, 19. 93.

Tickle, 86. (See Kittle.)

Toffer, lumber ; rubbish, 94.

Toggery, dress, 96.

Tooan, 86.

Topper, one of superior quality, 96.

Tosspots, drinking vessels ; drunkards, 39.

Towple, or Tipple, to turn head over heels, 96.

Tree, or Three, 86.

Tuck oot, a full meal, 5.

Tundher, 86.

Ugly, 87.

Undher-handed, not sufficient hands or employees, 91.

Van-jothery, miscellaneous collection, 92.

Vahjas, verjuice, 20.

Wackey, simpleton ; fool, 93.

Waffin, 87.

Wahdish, widish.

Wahk (1) ache, 87.

(2) work, 5. 33. 87.

Wahse-like, worse looking, 93.

Waintly, very much, 93.

Wakken, 5. 87.

Wallop, 30. 31. 38.

Wankle, 87.

Watty, simpleton, 46. 94. Another form of Wackey.

Wawey, languid ; feeble, 94.

Wayk, 43. 87.

Wax, 88.

Weeam, stomach, 92.

Web, the whole lot ; all of one kind, 93.

Wem, 88.

Whemmel'd doon, turned down, 39.

White Lady, a spectre, without a head, that haunts the Bail Welt at Skipsea Brough, and who destroys all fences on her "round," no matter how often or how strongly they are made, 33.

Wick, living, contraction of "quick," 39.

Wikes, corners of the mouth, 39.

Wot-sthreea, oat-straw, 39.

Wrang-ways, wrong way ; backwards, 93.

Wraxing, stretching; exaggerating, 94.

Yah, one, 47.

Yal, ale, 33. 34. 93.

Yan, one, 27. 33.

Yat (1), gate, 33. 94.; (2) hot, 92.

Yat-stowp, gate-post, 18. 51.

Yath, earth, 5. 47. 48. 94.

Yottan, a noise in the throat, produced by swallowing a large mouthful of liquid, 93.

Yowp, a loud shout, 38. 40. 65.

THOS. HOLDERNESS, PRINTER, DRIFFIELD.

This illustration of Speeton Beacon in 1886. is one of the six illustrations in Beacons of East Yorkshire. The post was removed in 1887, so that the Jubilee bonfire might be on its site. It fell into Vandal hands and was chopped up for firewood. Thus perished the last East Yorkshire beacon.

PRESS OPINIONS.—"A deeply interesting contribution to country history.—"Leeds Mercury." "Mr. Nicholson has rendered, in an extremely interesting .manner, a good service to future antiquarian students."—" Hull Miscellany." "Its pages represent more labour than has been expended on many a more pretentious treatise."—"Annandale Herald."

A few copies of FOLK MOOTS, post free for 6d, can be obtained only from the Author, 33, Leicester Street, Hull.

NORTH COUNTRY POETS:

POEMS AND BIOGRAPHIES

OF

NATIVES OR RESIDENTS OF NORTHUMBERLAND,
CUMBERLAND, WESTMORELAND, DURHAM,
LANCASHIRE, AND YORKSHIRE.

EDITED BY

WILLIAM ANDREWS, F.R.H.S.

Author of " Modern Yorkshire Poets," " Historic Yorkshire." Etc.

PRESS OPINIONS.

The following are a few of the Notices of the First Volume of this Book :—

" A collection of poems and biographical sketches, the first interest of which is only local, but which is so well made and so full of information that no limit need be set to its sphere, is Mr William Andrews' " North Country Poets." Mr Andrews is president of the Hull Literary Club, and has done much by a busy pen to bring into evidence the literary activity of his part of England. In this volume, which is the initial instalment of a fuller work, he begins a representative series of extracts from poems by natives or residents of Northumberland, Cumberland, Westmoreland, Durham, Lancashire, and Yorkshire. The selection shows care and good taste throughout. It includes poems by such writers as George Linnæus Banks, Mrs Browning, Arthur Clough, Sir Francis Doyle, Lord Houghton, Joseph Skipsey, Sir Henry Taylor, and Samuel Waddington—which partial enumeration may suffice to show the excellence of its matter. The biographical sketches make the book valuable for reference."—*The Scotsman.*

" The notices of the poets' writings are concisely and pleasantly penned, and most of capital critical merit, while the examples of poesy are admirably chosen." —*North London News.*

" It is a really excellent repository of the best local poetry of the Northern Counties, the specimens being selected with sound judgment, and the pithy biographies being in the case of each poet supplied by some writer well situated to obtain original and reliable information." *Lancashire Evening Post.*

www.ingramcontent.com/pod-product-compliance
Lightning Source LLC
Chambersburg PA
CBHW030624270326
41927CB00007B/1301